Nietzsche's Journey to Sorrento

Nietzsche's Journey to Sorrento

GENESIS OF THE PHILOSOPHY
OF THE FREE SPIRIT

Paolo D'Iorio

Translated by
Sylvia Mae Gorelick

The University of Chicago Press   Chicago & London

Paolo D'Iorio is director of research at the Centre National de la Recherche Scientifique and director of the HyperNietzsche project at the University of Munich. He is the author, editor, or coeditor of many books. **Sylvia Mae Gorelick** is a freelance translator and poet.

The University of Chicago Press, Chicago 60637
The University of Chicago Press, Ltd., London
© 2016 by The University of Chicago
All rights reserved. Published 2016.
Printed in the United States of America

25 24 23 22 21 20 19 18 17 16   1 2 3 4 5
ISBN-13: 978-0-226-16456-4 (cloth)
ISBN-13: 978-0-226-28865-9 (e-book)
DOI: 10.7208/chicago/9780226288659.001.0001

Originally published as Paolo D'Iorio, *Le voyage de Nietzsche à Sorrente*
© CRNS Éditions, 2012.

Library of Congress Cataloging-in-Publication Data

Names: D'Iorio, Paolo, author. | Gorelick, Sylvia Mae, translator.
Title: Nietzsche's journey to Sorrento : genesis of the philosophy of the free spirit / Paolo d'Iorio; translated by Sylvia Mae Gorelick.
Other titles: Voyage de Nietzsche à Sorrente. English
Description: Chicago : The University of Chicago Press, 2016. | Includes bibliographical references and index.
Identifiers: LCCN 2015041743 | ISBN 9780226164564 (cloth : alk. paper) | ISBN 9780226288659 (e-book)
Subjects: LCSH: Nietzsche, Friedrich Wilhelm, 1844–1900—Travel—Italy—Sorrento.
Classification: LCC B3316 .D5613 2016 | DDC 193—dc23 LC record available at http://lccn.loc.gov/2015041743

♾ This paper meets the requirements of ANSI/NISO Z39.48-1992 (Permanence of Paper).

To my grandfather
(Ischia 1898–Versilia 1986)

I don't have enough strength for the North: awkward and artificial souls reign there, who work as constantly and necessarily at the measures of prudence as the beaver at his dam. And to think that I spent my whole youth among them! That is what overcame me when, for the first time, I saw the evening come up, with its velvet gray and red, in the sky over Naples—like a shudder of pity for myself, that I had started my life by being old, and tears came to my eyes and the feeling of having been saved at the last moment.

I have enough spirit for the South.

FRIEDRICH NIETZSCHE, posthumous fragment
eKGWB/NF-1881,12 [181] (my translation)

CONTENTS

Becoming a Philosopher

The journey to Sorrento is not only Nietzsche's first great journey abroad, his first great journey to the South, but the decisive rupture in his life and the development of his philosophy. It happens in 1876, at a time when Nietzsche is suffering from serious moral and physical pain. His health is in decline; powerful neuralgias keep him bedridden at least once a week with unbearable migraines. It is also the time of an intellectual reassessment. At the age of thirty-two, Nietzsche begins to regret having accepted so young, too young perhaps, the professorship at Basel that he has held for seven years and which begins, now, to weigh upon him. Even more serious, the passion of his commitment as a Wagnerian propagandist is yielding gradually to disenchantment and doubt.

Four years earlier, the young professor of classical philology at the University of Basel had written a book titled *The Birth of Tragedy out of the Spirit of Music,* in which, beginning with an investigation into the origin of Greek tragedy, he proposed a reform of German culture founded on a metaphysics of art and the rebirth of tragic myth. According to this original combination of solid philological hypotheses with elements taken from Schopenhauer's philosophy and from the theory of the Wagnerian drama, the world can be justified only as an aesthetic phenomenon. The metaphysical principle that forms the essence of the world, which Nietzsche calls the "primordial-One" (*Ur-Eine*), is in eternal suffering because it is made up of a mixture of originary joy and pain. To free itself of this internal contradiction, it must create beautiful dream images. The world is the product of these anesthetic artistic representations, the reflection of a perpetual contradiction, the poetic invention of a suffering and tortured god. Even human beings, according to *The Birth of Tragedy*, are representations of the primordial-One, and when they produce artistic images such as Greek tragedy or the Wagnerian drama, they follow and magnify, in their turn, the saving dream-impulse of nature.[1] This metaphysical function of aesthetic activity explains the privileged position granted to the artist within the community insofar as he is the continuator of nature's finalities and the producer of myths that also favor social cohesion: "without myth every culture loses its healthy and creative natural force: only a horizon defined by myths circumscribes the entire movement of a culture in unity."[2] In the face of the modern world in disintegration, composed of a plurality of nonharmonized forces, Nietzsche had attempted, with this first book, to save civilization by placing it beneath the glass bell of myth and metaphysics and by entrusting it to the direction of the musical dramatist.[3]

The Wagnerian festival at Bayreuth, in August 1876, should have marked the beginning of this cultural action for a profound renewal of German culture and the birth of an artistic civilization. Nietzsche had invested great hope in this event, but it had disappointed him—he had judged it depressing and artificial.[4] From then on, he no longer believed in the possibility of a regeneration of German culture through the Wagnerian myth. His desire to put an end to his Wagnerian phase and to return to himself, to his philosophy and to his free thought, was strongest: "I am overcome with fear when I consider the uncertainty of the horizon of modern civilization. I praised, with some shame, the civilization beneath the glass bell. At last, I took courage and threw myself into the open sea of the world."[5]

It is at this time that his friend Malwida von Meysenbug invites him to spend a year in the South, not only to recover, but also to reflect on himself, as if to take a vacation from his own life. Nietzsche accepts right away. Thanks to the unexpected complicity of the journey and his illness, the philosopher returns to thinking. The journey distances him from the daily obligations of teaching, frees him from the habits and the weaknesses of everyday life, and removes him from the climate of the North. The illness forces him into rest, into *otium*, into waiting and patience . . . "But that is just what is called thinking! . . ."[6] In Sorrento, Nietzsche renounces his Wagnerian phase, recovers certain gains of his philosophical and philological training, and opens himself upon the thinking of modernity, of history, of science. Among the Sorrento papers, there is a very precise passage on this subject: "I want to declare expressly to the readers of my earlier works that I have abandoned the metaphysical-aesthetic views that essentially dominated them: they are pleasant, but untenable."[7]

In reality, even when he wrote *The Birth of Tragedy*, he was aware that the fascinating vision of the world that he was painting was only a beautiful illusion, which he himself hardly believed in. The first phase of Nietzsche's thought is, indeed, characterized by a profound divide between that which the young professor wrote publicly and that which he entrusted to his papers or to his students. This divide will be ended only with his journey to the South, when a whole flux of thoughts that had remained subterranean in relation to his public activity will finally spring forth into the light, giving the impression of a sudden change and arousing surprise and perplexity even among his close friends. It is in Sorrento that Nietzsche will write the majority of *Things Human, All Too Human*, the book dedicated to Voltaire that marks a turning point in his thought.[8] Through this book, Nietzsche will surpass the metaphysical and Wagnerian phase of his philosophy; because of it, he will lose nearly all of his friends who subscribe to the ideas of the Wagnerian movement: "I shall soon have to express ideas *regarded as disgraceful* by the one who nurtures them; then, even my friends and relations will become shy and frightened. I must pass through that fire. Then, I will belong to myself even more," he wrote before leaving.[9] Twelve years later, in the chapter of *Ecce Homo* devoted to "Things Human, All Too Human," Nietzsche will write of this radical change in his spiritual state in the following manner:

> What reached a decision in me at that time was not a break with Wagner. I noticed a total aberration of my instincts of which any particular blunder, whether it be called Wagner or the professorship at Basel, was only a symptom. I was overcome by *impatience* with myself; I saw that it was high time for me to recall and reflect on myself. All at once it became clear to me in a terrifying way how much time had already been wasted—how useless and arbitrary my whole existence as a philologist appeared in relation to my true task. I felt ashamed of this *false* modesty. . . Ten years lay behind me in which the *nourishment* of my spirit had come to a complete stop, in which I had learned nothing useful, in which I had forgotten an absurd amount in exchange for a mess of dusty erudition. Crawling scrupulously with bad eyes through the Greek metrists—that's what I had come to!—With commiseration, I saw myself utterly emaciated, utterly starved: my science entirely failed to include *realities*, and my "idealities"— who knows what the devil they were worth!—A truly burning thirst took hold of me: henceforth I pursued nothing other, in fact, than physiology, medicine, and natural sciences—even to properly historical studies I did not return until my *task* compelled me to, imperiously. It was then, too, that I first guessed the correlation between an activity chosen in defiance of one's instincts, a so-called "vocation" for which one does not have the *least* vocation, and the need for an

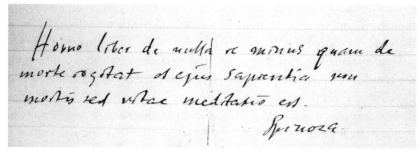

FIGURE 1: Spinoza in Nietzsche's Sorrento papers. Notebook U II 5, 57, Goethe-und Schiller-Archiv (GSA), 71/115.

anesthetization of the feeling of desolation and hunger by means of a narcotic art—for example, Wagnerian art.[10]

This first journey thus gives him the strength to abandon his professorship and transform his existence entirely. After his time in Sorrento, he will indeed attempt to return to Basel once more to teach; suffering, between life and death, he will try to return to the past, to regain the protection of his little Naumburg family. To no avail . . . for his true vocation calls him, now, to solitude, to the life of a wandering philosopher, to the South. In Sorrento, in the large bedroom on the third floor of the Villa Rubinacci, which looks out on an orange grove and, farther off, by the sea, onto Mount Vesuvius and the islands of the Gulf of Naples; in the luminous autumn afternoons, silent and orange-scented, still pervaded by midday sun and sea salt; during the evenings of reading aloud with friends, or during the day-trips to Capri or to the carnival in Naples; on walks through the little villages that extend along one of the most beautiful gulfs in the world, on this earth where the ancients believed they heard sirens; during the mornings spent writing the first aphorisms of his life, of which the drafts still carry the name *Sorrentiner Papiere* today, Nietzsche decides to become a philosopher.

From the terrace of his bedroom, facing Sorrento, Nietzsche can see the isle of Ischia: a volcanic island, a place both real and imaginary, and which will serve the philosopher as a model for the "blessed isles," the isles of Zarathustra's disciples. The blessed isles are those of the future, of hope, of youth. And this is exactly what Nietzsche recovers amid the torments of his illness: the visions, the plans, the promises of his youth. Not as vestiges of a henceforth buried past, but as voices that come out of the past to remind the despairing one who has lost his way of his life's future path. Ischia is not the island of

San Michele, the cemetery of the Venice lagoon and the model for the "isle of tombs" in *Zarathustra*: the silent isle of a decadent city in the middle of the sea of the lagoon that preserves and slowly decomposes everything. Ischia does not represent nostalgia and the memory of the past, but the place where volcanic subterranean forces penetrate the sea of forgetting to return into the light of the sun.

Not the twilight of a dying civilization, but the dawn of a new culture emerging above its three thousand years of history.

Between the ages of thirty-two and thirty-three, *in media vita*, in this tension between past and future, Nietzsche often dreams of his childhood, of the earlier eras of his life, "of people long forgotten or disappeared." The tangible sign that the time of his childhood was irretrievably past came to him with the news of the death of his "revered master," Friedrich Ritschl; of his maternal grandmother; and of his old colleague, the classical philologist at the University of Basel, Franz Gerlach. Philosophy, Schopenhauer affirmed, begins with a meditation on death. But among the *Sorrentiner Papiere* we find these enigmatic words of Spinoza: *Homo liber de nulla re minus quam de morte cogitat et ejus sapientia non mortis sed vitæ meditatio est*: The free man thinks of nothing less than death, and his knowledge is not a meditation on death but on life.[11]

CHAPTER ONE

Traveling South

To reconstruct this moment of such importance in Nietzsche's life, it will be necessary to consult the testimonies of the travelers who accompanied him on his way to the South. Indeed, because of his poor health and because his sight was severely weakened, Nietzsche left us only very few letters that might shed light on the proceedings of this transitional journey. But his traveling companions gave various testimonies, which will help us to grasp the atmosphere of this small circle of friends and to illuminate this period in Nietzsche's life from different perspectives. And yet, even if he writes few letters, the philosopher does not, for all that, give up writing or dictating his thoughts; by reading the notes that he jotted down in his notebooks, we will also follow the internal dialogue that he weaves with the authors who are dear to him. Thus our narration will follow two paths, making heard the voices of those who spoke of Nietzsche in their letters, and listening to the voice of the philosopher himself in the pages of his drafts.

The first of these figures who gravitated toward Nietzsche at that time is the countess Malwida von Meysenbug. A friend of Richard and Cosima Wagner, of Giuseppe Mazzini, of Gabriel Monod, of Romain Rolland . . . Malwida imagined herself, with her *Memoirs of an Idealist*, to be the educator of the German and European youth: "Her books," wrote Charles Andler, "drip with this tepid sentimentality, liquid and depthless. All of the 'idealists' without vigor, the discontented who, not daring to risk a real opposition, settled for a vague and elegant flight of the soul, flocked to her."[1] Sixty years old at the time, she belonged to the circle of Wagner's intimate friends and had met Nietzsche in 1872, when the first stone of the theater at Bayreuth was laid. It was also at

Bayreuth, during the festival of 1876, that she had conceived the idea of the journey to the South. She had first proposed Naples and then finally Sorrento as the ideal place to unite a small circle of friends.[2] Nearing the end of her long life, she recounts the preparation for this journey:

> I had been bound to Friedrich Nietzsche by the ties of a warm friendship since 1872, and at that time, his health had deteriorated to such a degree that he found it necessary to request a prolonged leave from the University of Basel in order to rest completely, for once. He felt drawn to the South. It seemed to this Greek parched for beauty that the blissful nature there would be able to cure him entirely. But he needed to be surrounded and cared for, and neither his mother nor his sister could accompany him. Since I had not yet established my residence in Rome, I wrote to him, proposing that he come with me to spend the winter in Sorrento, to seek rest, even recovery, in the lucky *dolce far niente* of the South. He responded: "Venerated friend, I really don't know how to thank you for what you propose to me in your letter; later, I will tell you *how* this word from you was said at the right time and how much more dangerous my condition would become without it; today I announce only that I will *come*." [. . .] I had taken a preparatory journey to Sorrento and found an apartment suitable for the little colony that we were to form after being only two. Namely, Nietzsche had invited one of his very dearest friends, Dr. Paul Rée, and one of his students, a young man from Basel named Brenner, to join us in Sorrento. I knew only the latter, who had come to Rome for his health, and, seeing no obstacle to this plan, I had looked for a house where we could all stay together. I found a vacant hotel in the middle of a vineyard, run by a German woman. On the second floor, there were bedrooms for the three men with terraces; on the third floor, bedrooms for me and my chambermaid, and a large living room for communal use. From the terraces there was a magnificent view beyond the flourishing foreground of the garden onto the Gulf and Mount Vesuvius, which was in full activity at the time and sent columns of smoke up to the sky in the evening.[3]

Malwida's account, written twenty years after the fact, is centered on her relationship with Nietzsche who, at the end of the century, had become one of the most famous and most quoted philosophers among his contemporaries—it is for this reason that Malwida neglects to mention that the stay in Sorrento had originally been organized not for Nietzsche but for Albert Brenner, a young man with fragile health, a student at the law school at the University of Basel and the philosopher's pupil.[4]

FIGURE 2: Malwida von Meysenbug. From Ernst Pfeiffer, ed., *Friedrich Nietzsche, Paul Rée, Lou von Salomé: die Dokumente ihrer Begegnung* (Frankfurt am Main: Insel-Verlag, 1970).

A STATELESS MAN'S PASSPORT

Nietzsche thus accepts Malwida's proposition and prepares for the journey. To travel to Italy, he needs a passport. But there is a problem: when he became a professor at the University of Basel, he had been forced to renounce his German citizenship, and in 1876, he had not yet been granted Swiss citizenship, which required eight years of uninterrupted residence. On September 29, 1876, the city of Basel thus issued him a special passport, a kind of safe-conduct valid for one year. However, it is this document that the philosopher will use until 1889. From a legal point of view, therefore, considering the fact that he will never regain his German citizenship, Nietzsche the traveler will be a stateless person for the rest of his life, moving throughout Europe with an expired passport that he will use only to withdraw money at the post office.[5] He will write, in 1881: "I have no passport and anyway, I have no use for one [...] My old passport from 1876 is still valid for the post office."[6] Apparently, in the era of rising nationalism, illegal immigrants moved through Europe more freely than today. In any case, this legal status of stateless philosopher seems to be particularly appropriate for the man who would place his hopes in the coming of the good Europeans of the future.

With his new passport in his pocket, Nietzsche begins his journey to the South with a two-week stop, from October 1 to 18, at the Hôtel du Crochet at Bex, in Switzerland. He is accompanied by a young philosopher, Paul Rée, who will play an important role in the stay in Sorrento and in this phase of Nietzsche's philosophy.

> I have been in Bex for eight days and am enjoying the beautiful autumn in the company of Rée, the incomparable. Yet I had to stay in bed for a day and a half with the most violent pains (they lasted from Monday at noon until Tuesday night, over thirty hours). The day before yesterday and yesterday the first stages of a new attack began, which I'm expecting tomorrow. This place and the stop at the Hôtel (where Rée and I are staying alone in an annex) are exceptionally beautiful. From seven to eight o'clock (before sunrise), I take a walk. Likewise from four-thirty to seven o'clock, after sunset: during the day, I sit on the terrace in front of our rooms.
> —October 18, journey to the South.[7]

A year later, in a letter to Nietzsche, Rée will remember this stay in the little annex at the Hôtel du Crochet, measured by walks, resting, and reading, and where Nietzsche had celebrated, on October 15, his thirty-second birthday.

Valable pour *un an*.

PASSE · PORT.

Confédération Suisse.

CANTON DE BALE-VILLE.

SIGNALEMENT.

Age *31 ans*

Taille de mes. suisse.
- pieds *cinq*
- pouces *sept*
- lignes *neuf*

1 pied de Suisse a 10 poures, le pouce 10 lignes; le pied de Suisse contient 30 centimètres de France.

Cheveux *brunsclairs*
Sourcils *dito*
Front *haut*
Yeux *bruns*
Nez *proport.*
Bouche *moyenne*
Menton *ovale*
Barbe *brunclair*
Figure *ovale*

Signes particuliers.

Signature du porteur:

Dr Friedrich Nietzsche
Professeur

Nous B'urguemestre et Conseil d'État du Canton de Bâle - Ville en Suisse

prions les autorités civiles et militaires de laisser passer sûrement et librement

Monsieur Nietzsche (Frédéric)

Dr et Professeur à l'Université de Bâle,

et de lui prêter aide et assistance en cas de besoin.

Fait à BALE ce *29 Septembre 1876.*

pour Le Secrétaire d'État:

Gottisheim P.

FIGURE 3: Nietzsche's provisional passport. Staatsarchiv Basel-Stadt, Erziehungakten CC 15, 16, from David Marc Hoffmann, ed., *Nietzsche und der Schweiz*: 1994, 169.

FIGURE 4: Paul Rée. Photograph: Raffello Ferretti, Naples, 1876–1877, GSA 101/385.

Paul Rée will even regard this time as "the honeymoon of their friendship": "These days, my thoughts wander toward Bex and have no desire to be called back to the present. It was, as it were, the honeymoon of our friendship, and the little house apart, the wooden balcony, the clusters of grapes, and The Wise Man complete the picture of a perfect situation."[8]

In the peacefulness of these two weeks in Bex, Nietzsche had returned to his notes on the liberation of the spirit that were to form the basis of a fifth *Untimely Meditation*. He even announces to his sister Elisabeth that the text of this *Meditation* is already finished and that he is only missing someone to whom to dictate it in order to send it to the publisher. On October 18, the two friends prepare for the journey toward Genoa where a boat for Naples awaits them: "Beloved sister, it's the day of our departure, the foehn blows a very southerly wind. It's hard to believe that I'll be as happy in the South as in Bex. The choice was excellent!"[9]

Shortly before the departure, in response to a telegram from Wagner sent from Venice, Nietzsche had written: "When I think of you in Italy, I remember that the inspiration for the beginning of *Rheingold* came to you there. May it always remain a land of beginnings for you! [. . .] You know, perhaps, that I am also going to Italy next month, to find the land not of beginnings, but of the end of my suffering."[10] In reality, as we shall see, the physical suffering will not end, but the journey to Italy will mark, for Nietzsche, the birth of a new cycle of thought.

NIGHT TRAIN THROUGH MONT CENIS

Nietzsche and Rée make their next stop in Geneva, at the Hôtel de la Poste, where Albert Brenner meets them. At nine in the evening, Nietzsche and Brenner take the night train, which carries them to Genoa on the afternoon of October 20, while Rée, who had prolonged his stay in Geneva, will only arrive in Genoa during that night. Nietzsche writes a telegraphic-style report of the journey to his mother and his sister: "Bad departure from Bex; in Geneva, a bit better; at lunchtime ate at the Hôtel de la Poste. Brenner arrived. Night journey through Mont-Cenis, afternoon the next day, arrived in Genoa with a severe headache: immediately to bed, vomiting, and duration of this state 44 hours. Today, Sunday, better; just now returned from a trip to the port and the sea. Beautiful silence and colors of the evening. Tomorrow (Monday) evening departure on the steamboat to Naples, we three friends have decided together on a sea journey. Warmest regards to you both."[11]

Not a word in this postcard about a strange meeting in the night train with the baroness Claudine von Brevern and Isabelle von der Pahlen. The latter, however, was so overwhelmed by her meeting with Nietzsche that she would give a detailed description of it in her 1902 book devoted to the philosopher, lyrically evoking this "great stranger," this "Croesus of thought who had worlds to give." This is how Isabelle von der Pahlen relates what she considers as one of the most extraordinary experiences of her life:

It was in Geneva, on a soft October evening in the year of grace 1876 that the long-cherished desire for a stay in Italy was fulfilled. Under the protection of a friend of my mother's, I cheerfully boarded a first-class compartment, which promised us a night of refreshing rest, for it was empty except for a masculine shape, leaning motionless in a corner. Thanks to her comfortable down cushion, my companion soon fell into a peaceful slumber, while I wore myself out with my preparations for sleep. My father, in his loving care, had given me an air cushion, which I tried in vain to inflate. Absorbed in my love's labor's lost, I suddenly catch sight of a finger approaching the rubber monster.

Weary of my battle with the object, I give up on my efforts and say, laughing: "Please, see if you can help me, if you have more breath than I." The great stranger seizes the spineless shell and tries in vain to breathe his spirit into it.

We give it up, both decide against sleep, and spend the night in lively conversation: a true orgy of thoughts, which left me with the freshest and most luminous memory, often brought to my mind as one of the most singular experiences of my life.

What did we chat about during those unforgettable hours? Of each and every thing that exists between heaven and earth, of art and science, of the heights and depths of existence, with the exception of all personal circumstances. I know that I was literally intoxicated by the power and novelty of the ideas that sprang from the lips of the man who sat facing me in such astonishing abundance and original manifestations. A Croesus of thought who had worlds to give and who was in just the right mood to do it. [. . .]

My partner carried La Rochefoucauld's *Maxims* with him, to which the first threads of our conversation were tied. He praised the gift of the French, La Rochefoucauld, Vauvenargues, Condorcet, Pascal, for sharpening a thought so much that it could compete with a medal in acuity and relief. He also spoke of the roughness of the content, which, through the application of the most difficult form, attains artistic perfection. He supported this claim through the following verses, which, by their impact, have remained in my ears:

> Oui, l'œuvre sort plus belle
> D'une matière au travail rebelle—
> Vers, marbre, onyx, émail—
> Point de contraires fausses,
> Mais que pour marcher droit—
> Muse, tu chausses,
> Un cothurne étroit[12]

(I later found this stanza in Théophile Gautier's *Émaux et Camées*—his motto is: "Le buste survivra à la cité."[13])

In these words lies the formative principle of his aphoristic style. But at the same time they contain the conviction of the first artist of language, beside Goethe and Heine, that the German tongue is an extremely rough material, on the same level as stone and ore.

From the subject of social problems, my companion now began to speak of religious and philosophical things, of which my humble intelligence must, after all, have attained a considerable understanding, for I remember that he asked me, quite unexpectedly, this question: "Is it not so, miss, that you too are a freethinker [*Freigeist*]?"

I protested against this designation as a translation of the term "*esprit fort*" ["strong spirit"] which, invented in the last quarter of the eighteenth century by the encyclopedists, carries a strongly polemic connotation, and added: "My wish is to be a 'free spirit' ['*freier Geist*'], which could, if necessary, correspond to the '*libre penseur*' ['freethinker'] of the French."

At this point he made a note in his pocket book, as he had often done over the course of our conversation. I remembered this later, in 1880, when, on the first page of *Things Human, All Too Human*, the subtitle "A Book for Free Spirits" sent me vividly back to that hour. I regarded this second title as a dedication in which I also had my part, and I relished the work as a magnificent commentary, containing the entire world, of our dialogue on that soft Italian night.[14]

It is more than likely that Isabelle exaggerates the importance of her nighttime conversation in the train from Geneva to Genoa for the genesis of *Things Human, All Too Human*, which had been published in 1878. In reality, the idea of a book on the free spirit came long before this meeting. From 1870, one of the first titles that Nietzsche had given to what would later become *The Birth of Tragedy* was *Tragedy and Free Spirits*. This first title bore witness to an intention to connect the Eleusinian wisdom of the Wagnerian music drama with the philosopher's freedom of spirit and, in perspective, to open a dimension proper to the philosophical genius of the new culture of Bayreuth.[15] But the artistic genius had ended up occupying the whole stage as well as the entirety of Nietzsche's notebooks and writings, at the expense of the freedom of the philosophical spirit. Yet after the festival at Bayreuth, Nietzsche returns, this time in full force, to his meditations on the free spirit, inspired in part by a rereading of Montaigne's *Essais*.[16] In particular, a diary of 1876 can be regarded as the true "notebook of the free spirit": this is very likely the notebook that Isabelle watched fill with notations in the train to Italy.

FIGURE 5 : Isabelle von der Pahlen in 1876–1877. Goethe-und Schiller-Archiv, 101/365.

This notebook contains twenty fragments that directly concern "the way *toward* the freedom *of the spirit*" and judge that "a man who thinks freely experiences the evolution of entire generations ahead of time."[17] It is affirmed here that the free spirit lives for the future of man, inventing new possibilities of existence and weighing the old ones. These fragments divide humanity into free men and slaves: "the man who does not have two-thirds of his day to himself is a slave, no matter what else he may be: statesman, businessman, official, scholar."[18] It is also a matter of the way to make life easy and light: "Every man has his *recipes* for enduring life (partly to let it be easy, partly to make it easy, if it has once revealed itself as hard), even the criminal. This art of living applied everywhere must be reconstructed. Explain what the recipes of *religion* actually achieve. Not to lighten life but to take life lightly. Many want to make it *harder* in order to offer afterwards *their supreme recipes* (art, asceticism, etc.)."[19] The conclusion of the book, which was to be called *Das leichte Leben, The Light Life*, had to connect the freedom of spirit and love of truth to life made light and easy according to the double-meaning of *leicht* in German: "We can live like the gods who live lightly if we learn to stand before the truth in vivid rapture [. . .] In conclusion: free spirits are gods *who live lightly*."[20] Other fragments reveal the desired effect of these meditations on the reader: "Goal: to put the reader in such an elastic state that he stands on his tiptoes [. . .] Free thought, fairy tales, lasciviousness lift man onto his tiptoes."[21] This whole set of motives will be used later for the composition of key aphorisms in *Things Human, All Too Human*, such as number 225:

Free spirit a relative concept. —He is called a free spirit who thinks differently from what, on the basis of his origin, environment, his class and profession, or on the basis of the dominant views of his time, would have been expected of him. He is the exception, the bounded spirits are the rule; the latter reproach him that his free principles either originate in a desire to shock and offend or eventuate in free actions, that is to say in actions incompatible with bounded morals. Occasionally it is also said that this or that free principle is to be attributed to perversity and mental overexcitation; but this is merely the voice of malice, which does not believe what it says but desires only to wound: for the superior quality and sharpness of his intellect is usually written on the face of the free spirit in characters clear enough even for the bounded spirit to read. But the two other derivations of free thought are honestly meant; and many free spirits do in fact emerge in one or other of these ways. But for this reason, the principles they arrive at along these paths could still be truer and more reliable than those of the bounded spirits. In the case of the knowledge of truth, the point is that one *possesses* it, not from what impetus one sought it or on which paths one found it. If the free spirits are right, the bounded spirits are wrong, regardless of whether the former have arrived at the truth by way of immorality or the latter have hitherto cleaved to untruth out of morality. —In any event, however, it is not inherent to the free spirit's nature to have the more correct opinions but, rather, to have liberated himself from tradition, whether successfully or unsuccessfully. As a rule, though, he will nonetheless have the truth on his side, or at least the spirit of the search for truth: he demands reasons, the others, beliefs.[22]

The difference between the free spirit and the *esprit fort* is also thematized in a note from the notebook of the free spirit to be developed thereafter in aphorism 230 of *Things Human, All Too Human*:

Esprit fort. —Compared with him who has tradition on his side and requires no reasons for his actions, the free spirit is always weak, especially in actions; for he knows too many motives and points of view and therefore has an unsure and unpracticed hand. What means are there, now, of making him nonetheless *relatively strong*, so that he can at least make his way and not ineffectually perish? How does the strong spirit (*esprit fort*) emerge? This, in the individual case, is the question of how genius is produced. Whence comes the energy, the inflexible force, the endurance with which the individual thinks, in opposition to tradition, to attain a wholly individual knowledge of the world?[23]

But let us return to young Isabelle's pages. After the intimate philosophical conversation of the night, the light of day now bathes the two travelers' compartment as the train approaches Italy:

A beautiful sunlit day dawned only too early; my companion, Mrs. Claudine von Brevern awoke and, after reciprocal presentations, the conversation lost its stimulating nature of intimacy and incognito.

Once we arrived in Genoa, we continued on to the same hotel, an old palace near the port, and spent several days there in close communication with the professor at Basel, at that time unknown outside of specialists and the circle of Wagnerians. Yet he showed himself only the next day. As I later deduced from an allusion of his companion, Paul Rée, his sensitive nerves had had to overwork to pay the price of that exalted night. And due to a headache, he had to forgo the trip to the Villa Pallavicini that we had arranged together. This prevented the three of us from taking many beautiful excursions together,

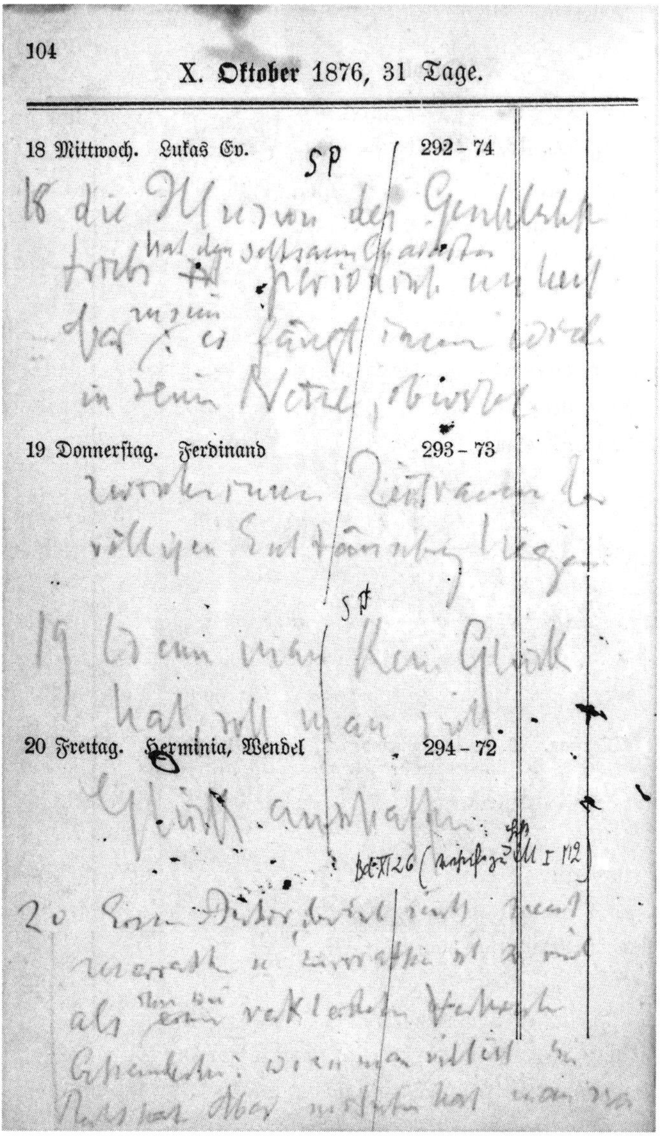

X. **Oktober** 1876, 31 Tage.

18 Mittwoch. Lukas Ev.   292 – 74

19 Donnerstag. Ferdinand   293 – 73

20 Freitag. Herminia, Wendel   294 – 72

FIGURE 6: The notes that Nietzsche wrote in his notebook of the free spirit during his train journey to Genoa. Notebook N II 1, 203, GSA 71/173.

including a long nighttime walk through the picturesque streets and alleys of Genoa, which stands as a luminous point in my memory.

Nietzsche's words made the past of Genoa come colorfully and vividly alive before our minds' eyes. He opened up our understanding of the Renaissance and Baroque art that left their mark upon "Genova, la superba," the city of palaces and Venice's old rival. [. . .] How ineffably the pleasure of this picturesque place was intensified when, from the magic of the present, Nietzsche's eloquence evoked the shadows of those powerful ancient times![24]

The travelers were obliged to say goodbye by letter, for Nietzsche, suffering a new migraine attack, could not come to the meeting that had been arranged with the two ladies. He apologized in a small note addressed to the baroness von Brevern:

> Pardon me, dear lady, for letting you down and for being unable to fulfill my promise (or rather my *desire*). Pardon a half-invalid! On the way to the train station, where I was going with Dr. Rée, I suddenly felt so weak and frail that I had to turn back, ashamed and reluctant as a vanquished army. Yet before my departure I cannot fail to express to you in writing my joy at a meeting that has allowed me to see a double play: a *high degree* of culture and a high aspiration to culture.
>
> My most sincere wishes to you and to Fräulein von der Pahlen and my highest regards for your journey.[25]

Later converted to graphology, Isabelle von der Pahlen would reproduce this small note in her book *Nietzsche in the Mirror of his Writing*, as proof that Nietzsche displayed great control over his physical pains, concluding that he was a wise man rather than an intellectualist philosopher. . . .

THE CAMELS OF PISA

As chance would have it, however, the professor and the two ladies met again the next day, October 24, in Pisa. Indeed, Nietzsche, taking advantage of the steamboat's stop in Livorno, had thought of taking a brief excursion to the city of the leaning tower, where the two friends, who had arrived by train, were already taking a coach ride. We hear again from the enthusiastic Isabelle:

> I shouted for joy when I caught sight of Nietzsche, walking mournfully along his path: "All alone, professor? Climb in with us then, we're taking the same route."

Nietzsche accepted instantly and together the three of us went to see the dome, the baptistery, and the *Campo Santo* in the joyful, drunken mood that had infected my companions. Rarely was Orcagna's masterpiece *The Last Judgment* contemplated in such a state. I must confess honestly that many traces of sublimity escaped me while the grotesque scenes, especially two demons dragging a fat monk into an abyss, did not fail to make their impression.

As a critic of Catholic mythology, Nietzsche revealed a whole new side of his personality, radiantly mocking and sarcastic, glistening in all colors.

We were received at the train station by Nietzsche's traveling companion, Paul Rée, with whom I had not yet exchanged ten words: he was visibly upset. Rather agitated, he took me aside and blatantly expressed his displeasure to me for having driven Nietzsche into an excited, nervous, and thus harmful state in spite of his efforts. [. . .] I then learned from Rée, the faithful Achates, that his friend required great calm and solitude to combat a severe nervous condition.[26]

Yet Rée's intervention did not prevent the young professor and the young baroness from continuing their conversation. But soon the train for Livorno arrives, the friends say goodbye, and the journey to the South begins again. It is probably on the occasion of this short trip that Nietzsche saw the camels of the domain of San Rossore, which he would remember three years later, in the dialogue between the wanderer and his shadow that opens the second volume of *Things Human, All Too Human*:

THE SHADOW: As it is so long since I heard you speak, I would like to give you the opportunity to do so.

THE WANDERER: Someone is speaking: —where? and who? It almost seems as though it were myself speaking, though in an even weaker voice than mine.

THE SHADOW (after a pause): Are you not glad to have the opportunity to speak?

THE WANDERER: By God and all the things I do not believe in, my shadow is speaking; I hear it but I do not believe it.

THE SHADOW: Let us accept it and think no more about it: in an hour it will all be over.

THE WANDERER: That is just what I thought when, in a wood near Pisa, I saw first two and then five camels.[27]

This day was precisely the 24th of October 1876. These camels had been introduced into San Rossore around the end of the seventeenth century by the

(Ed.** Alinari) N.º 19299. PISA — R. Tenuta di S. Rossore. ,Cammelli, al pascolo.

FIGURE 7 : The camels of Pisa in the early twentieth century. Alinari/Roger Viollet.

Grand Duke Cosimo III de' Medici. Informally referred to as "camels," they were in fact dromedaries that were raised in the park of San Rossore up until the end of the sixties. The last specimen died in 1976, a hundred years after Nietzsche's journey.[28]

NAPLES: FIRST REVELATION OF THE SOUTH

Finally, at one o'clock in the morning on Wednesday, October 25, the three friends arrive in Naples, where Malwida von Meysenbug is waiting for them, and they go to the *Pension allemande* of Chiatamone. Albert Brenner, Nietzsche's young student, testifies to the adventurous circumstances of the arrival in a letter to his family:

> We arrived at the port last night (Wednesday), at one o'clock in the morning and were foolish enough to push on to Naples instead of staying on the ship. We therefore found ourselves in a narrow boat, rowed by four sailors from the port. It was a dark night, no sound could be heard any longer except for several incomprehensible words exchanged now and then between our suspicious

oarsmen. I began to see ghosts and gripped my dagger under my cloak, cursing the elegance of my top hat, which I would have readily seen at the bottom of the sea. We landed in a small, secluded port illuminated by hardly any light. Several seaside customs officers approached us, looking even more like thieves, and demanded a tip. Then the four oarsmen divided up our two suitcases and dragged them along the narrow street that leads to Chiatamone, the *Pension allemande*, where we were going. Nietzsche, Rée, and I had to oversee our luggage carriers: they walked at a distance of around twenty to thirty paces from one another. I hardly doubted that they were leading us astray, to some remote boutique in order to abduct us—I really had more curiosity than fear, and a quiet resignation—but my coat with flaring sides, which gave me a bandit-like look, our sunken eyes, and our exhaustion all lent us something unsettling anyway, and we arrived safe and sound. Miss von Meysenbug is here. She has put a great deal of effort into arranging everything for the best. Tomorrow we leave for Sorrento.[29]

The following day, however, the four friends remain in Naples and find the time to take a long coach ride in the city's streets, which Nietzsche will remember later. For the moment, Malwida is the one who, in a letter to her adoptive daughter, captures the magic of Nietzsche's ecstatic contact with the South:

> On the evening of the day before yesterday, I traveled through Posillipo in a coach with my three gentlemen; the light was divine, truly fairylike, Mount Vesuvius was majestically crowned with thunderclouds, and from the flames and the gloomy black-red glow there rose a rainbow. The city gleamed as if made of gold while on the other side, the deep blue sea extended; the sky, covered with bright, glistening clouds was translucent green and blue and the glorious islands stood among the waves as in a fairy tale. It was so marvelous that the gentlemen were as if drunk from ecstasy. I have never seen Nietzsche so lively. He laughed for joy.[30]

Alluding to this episode in her *Memoirs*, Malwida will once again remember "how Nietzsche's face lit up with a joyful astonishment that was nearly childlike, how he was overcome with emotion; finally he burst into exalted exclamations on the South, which I welcomed as a good omen for his stay."[31]

Nietzsche wrote little during this time period because of his eye pains, and no direct testimony has remained of his vivid impressions on the arrival in Naples, in the *mezzogiorno* of Italy. But five years later, in the autumn of 1881, we find, in one of his work notebooks, three brief notes that speak precisely of

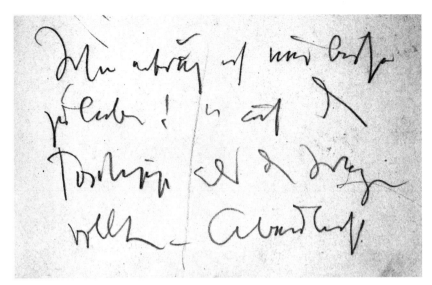

F I G U R E   8 : "'Wie ertrug ich nur bisher zu leben!' auf dem Posilipp als der Wagen rollte—Abendlicht." Notebook N V 7, 120, GSA 71/197.

this first revelation of the magic of the South, as the sunset over Posillipo had suddenly opened his eyes: for the first time, he realized that Northern Europe had exhausted his entire youth, but also that he had enough spirit to begin a new life in the South.[32]

> How have I merely endured living until now! in Posillipo while the car rolled—evening light.
>
> Posillipo and all the blind whose eyes will be opened.
>
> I don't have enough strength for the North: awkward and artificial souls reign there, who work as constantly and necessarily at the measures of prudence as the beaver at his dam [*crossed out in the manuscript:* Northern Europe is full of them]. And to think that I spent my whole youth among them! That is what overcame me when, for the first time, I saw the evening come up, with its velvet gray and red, in the sky over Naples [*crossed out in the manuscript:* you had been dying without having seen that]—like a shudder of pity for myself, that I had started my life by being old, and tears came to my eyes and the feeling of having been saved at the last moment.
>
> I have enough spirit for the South.[33]

CHAPTER TWO

"The School of Educators" at the Villa Rubinacci

The South that stood before Nietzsche's eyes for the first time was embodied in the form of Sorrento, a small fishing village that was beginning to attain a certain touristic popularity and which had been the destination of renowned travelers. It was the hometown of Tasso, Giacomo Casanova had come to the city in 1771 after one of his love affairs, James Cooper in 1829, John Ruskin in 1842, Alexis de Tocqueville in 1850–1851, Louise Collet in 1860, Ferdinand Gregorovius in 1864, Hippolyte Taine in 1864. . . .[1]

Wagner and his family had been staying in the magnificent rooms of the Hôtel Vittoria since October 5, where they sought respite from the fatigue and disillusionment of the first festival at Bayreuth. For their part, the group composed of Malwida and her chambermaid Trina, Nietzsche, Rée, and Brenner, arrived on October 27 and moved into a small hotel, the Villa Rubinacci, slightly outside the village. But let us allow the travelers to speak, who, just having arrived, hurry to describe their new surroundings to their families. Malwida will inform her foster daughter Olga of the search for accommodations:

> After much reflection, we decided to go to Sorrento; thus, we left yesterday morning and arrived here in the glorious weather. We then came to the *pension allemande*, the Villa Rubinacci, which I had already seen quite recently[2] and where the gentlemen were so happy that they decided to stay right away. The place is, indeed, very beautiful and includes the convenience that the gentlemen have their own quarters, such that I am utterly unbothered by them. The Wagners, whom we visited yesterday evening, were angry that we didn't take

F I G U R E   9 : The piazza in Sorrento, circa 1876. From Alessandro Fiorentino, *Memorie di Sorrento* (Napoli: Electa, 1991), 115 (photo Ziegler).

one of the houses neighboring their hotel, which is very sunny, but that would have been more expensive and less independent. Here, we are our own masters and the German landlady is a perfectly humble creature. Trina is in full activity; she is pampering the gentlemen and arranging the rooms. There are terraces on all sides of the house. The sitting room windows open onto sun-drenched Naples, my beloved Ischia, and Vesuvius. In front of the house, there is a true forest of olive and orange trees, which forms the foreground of greenery in the painting.[3]

Albert Brenner, after evoking the magnificent coach ride in Posillipo ("where Naples was truly a miracle") and the hour-and-a-half-long journey to Sorrento "down the street that runs along the sea," extends his description to the town itself:

We are living slightly outside of Sorrento, in this part of the city where there are only gardens, villas, and greenhouses. The whole neighborhood is like a cloister. The streets are narrow, wedged between interminable walls, twice the height of a man and beyond which lie orange trees, cypresses, fig trees, and garlands of grapes, which make the blue streak of sky the most beautiful setting. Most of the sparse houses are inside enclosures, such that one has the feeling of being in a labyrinth. There are real mule paths.

Sorrento itself is a quarter of an hour away. In the middle of the city, near the "piazza" there is a bridge that extends over a deeply romantic ravine. There is a little marina in the small town below. It seems that aristocracy live there too. Bit by bit, we will surely see everything.

We ourselves are living in the "Villa Rubinacci." On one side, it looks onto the sea, the isle of Ischia, and Vesuvius. One can see this view all day long, in all degrees of illumination. On the other side, we see a narrow mule path. A small orange grove separates us from the sea. From this grove, one must go down nearly vertically; Sorrento is on a cliff.

Today is a holiday and also the first day of autumn, although everything is still green and pleasant and no straw carpets have been laid out yet. My windows are open as I write to you. We have two large terraces, which look onto the sea and the mountains. In spite of all this, the house is not only relatively but extremely cheap; it is not an elegant villa: for example, elegant villas don't have rugs as good as ours and, anyhow, every farmhouse has stone floors and terraces.[4]

This time, Nietzsche too takes up his pen and celebrates the move to Sorrento in a note to his sister on October 28:

Here we are in Sorrento! The journey from Bex took eight days: in Genoa I was ill, from there the sea journey took us about three days and, imagine, we escaped seasickness. Anyway, I prefer this mode of traveling to those terrible train journeys. We met Miss von Meysenbug in a hotel in Naples and yesterday we came to our new homeland, the Villa Rubinacci, Sorrento, *près de Nâples* [*sic*].[5]

I have a very large room with a high ceiling and a terrace. I just came back from my first swim in the sea. According to Rée, the water was warmer than the northern sea in July. Last night we went to see the Wagners, who are living five minutes from here, at the Hôtel Vittoria, and will stay through November.

Sorrento and Naples are beautiful, it is not an exaggeration. The air here is a mixture of mountain and sea air. It is truly beneficent for the eyes: just in front of my terrace, I have a great green garden below me (which stays green even in the winter), and behind it the very dark sea, and behind that Vesuvius. Let us hope. In all love and faithfulness, your F.[6]

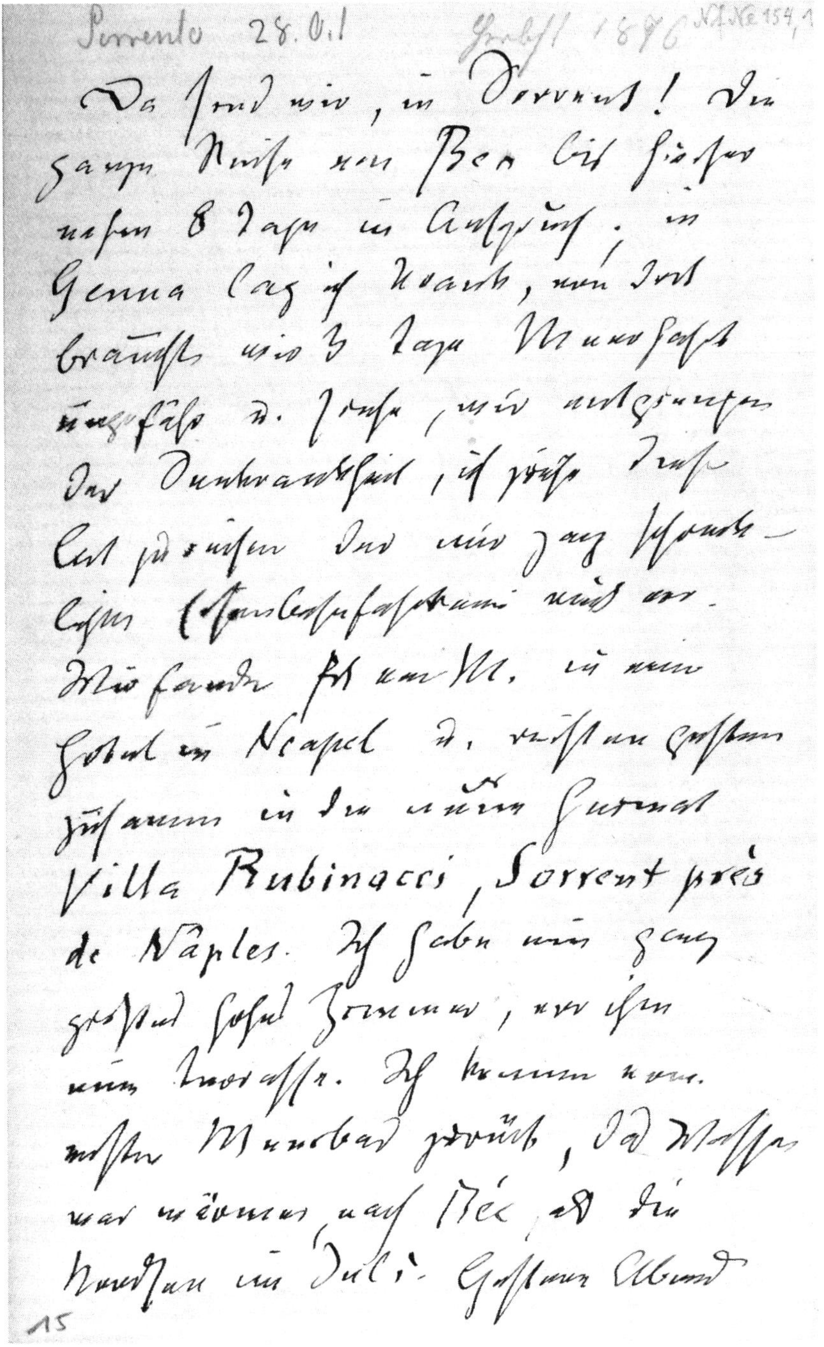

FIGURE 10: Nietzsche's first letter to his sister from Sorrento. October 28, 1876, GSA 71/ BW-271,9.

FIGURE 11: Richard and Cosima Wagner in 1872. From Manfred Eger, *"Alle 5000 Jahre glückt es"* (Tutzing: Schneider, 2010).

RICHARD WAGNER IN SORRENTO

At the end of the first festival at Bayreuth, on the verge of leaving for Southern Italy to rest, Richard and Cosima Wagner continued to reflect on this artistic event, so lengthily awaited and prepared for, and whose influence they had not yet managed to grasp. Cosima wrote in her diary: "*September 9* Departure of Mathilde Maier—the last visitor. After that preparations for the journey. In the evening a long discussion about the performances and the experience gained

F I G U R E   1 2 : The Hôtel Vittoria in Sorrento in 1890. From Fiorentino, 164 (photo Sommer).

during them. [. . .] Costumes, scenery, everything must be done anew for the repeat performances. Richard is very sad, says he wishes he could die!"[7] After a journey through Verona, Venice, Bologna, and Naples, the Wagners finally settle in Sorrento:

> *Thursday, October 5* Sorrento, Hôtel Vittoria, we have taken the little cottage beside the hotel, wonderful peace.
>
> *Tuesday, October 10* Spent the afternoon on the splendid terrace, from which one looks out over an olive grove and the sea.
>
> *Saturday, October 14* This spot here is becoming increasingly dear to me; the paths between two walls with overhanging trees, the ravines and rocks, the olive trees, it has all become so familiar to me, and I also hear nothing upsetting here. Only Richard's worries can hardly be banished, even for a few moments, and so the horizon is clouded.
>
> *Thursday, October 26* A wonderful drive in the afternoon, visited all the grottoes between Meta and Sorrento, thinking of Dante and Doré; splendid sky, the island lying blissfully before us in a golden light, Vesuvius with the villages on its slopes, reddish-gray and brownish-gold, somberly threatening. From Meta, home on foot, a long walk in the moonlight; everything looking

wonderful, the houses as much as the gardens with their tall stone-pines, those aristocrats among trees. In the evening we are indeed somewhat tired, but in splendid spirits. I feel as if life has granted me a respite here!"[8]

Yet the beauty of the places and the feeling of respite did not dispel the worries of the Wagner couple. Indeed, sadness and doubts, the awareness of the great hiatus between the dream and its realization, the regret of the past and the anguish for the future will make up the true leitmotif of their stay in Sorrento. On October 18, Cosima writes in her diary: "Frequent thoughts of giving up the festival entirely and disappearing,"[9] and November 5: "In the evening, conversation with Richard, during which I try to talk about all sorts of strange things, but we always come back to the one dismal subject. Richard says that his main feeling during the performances was, 'Never again, never again!' He winced so much, he says, that the King [Ludwig II of Bavaria] asked him what was the matter, and then he had to restrain himself forcibly."[10] Even from a financial point of view the festival had been a failure and the Wagner couple seriously considered paying their debts, giving up the theater, and leaving the stage.

On October 15, Nietzsche's birthday, Cosima had thrown herself once more into reading the philosopher's fourth *Untimely Meditation*: *Richard Wagner in Bayreuth*. In this writing of July 1876, Nietzsche had composed a portrait of the maestro, of his dreams and youthful utopias, of his conception of music, and of the role of theater in a profoundly renewed society and had put his whole intellectual process under the sign of fidelity. As Mazzino Montinari[11] has shown, this *Untimely Meditation* is a very skillful mosaic of hidden quotations, taken, in fact, from the composer's early theoretical writings. It thus worked as a magic mirror turned toward Bayreuth and toward Wagner himself, on which the following question was engraved: was this festival of jaded nobles really the faithful expression of the dream that had driven Wagner's entire life, since his Feuerbachian writings in the spirit of 1848 such as *Art and Revolution* and *The Artwork of the Future*? From that point on, Nietzsche no longer believed it and the maestro knew it. Before the festival, Nietzsche's writing appeared to be the manifesto of a renewed Wagnerism; after this society event, attended by crowned heads and jaded nobles, it merely made the philosopher's disillusionment more painful. It is significant that Nietzsche, who was still in Bex on October 15, celebrated his thirty-second birthday writing aphorisms on the free spirit with his new friend Paul Rée. Everyone has his own way of overcoming deception: Cosima turned toward the past, Nietzsche was already looking toward the future. As for the maestro Richard Wagner, he would overcome this period of depression by returning to a project begun

FIGURE 13: The terrace of the Hôtel Vittoria in 1875. From Fiorentino, 166 (photo Rive).

in 1845, and which he had traced out many times over the following years, particularly in a moment of vivid inspiration, on Good Friday 1857, during a trip through the area surrounding the lake of Zurich: to write a holy drama on the figure of Parsifal. Far from going back to Feuerbach, Wagner went from Schopenhauerian metaphysics to the Christian religion.

It is in this psychological state that Wagner and Nietzsche meet for the last time in Sorrento. In the meantime, the Wagners have moved from their annex to the third floor of the Hôtel Vittoria and it is there that Malwida, Nietzsche, and Rée visit them on the evening of October 27th, the very day of their arrival. Cosima writes in her diary: "Nice day, bathing with the children. In the afternoon took a little walk with Richard and the children, then sat for a long time with Richard on our terrace and looked at the sea. After that a visit from Malwida, Dr. Rée, and our friend Nietzsche, the latter very run down and much concerned with his health. They are staying in Sorrento."[12] After the visit, the Wagner couple lingers on the terrace, writing and reflecting before the scene of the sea and the olive groves surrounding the hotel. In a troubling contemporaneity, the very same evening of Nietzsche's arrival in Sorrento, the couple meditates upon the passion of Jesus Christ, as Cosima's diary indicates:

Friday, October 27 Moonlight over the olive garden, thought of Christ: "If it be possible, let this cup pass from me; nevertheless not as I will, but as thou wilt"—the epitome of all suffering and all salvation; how often does the soul beseech that the cup may pass, how hard to submit, and how seldom does it succeed in doing so! But when it does succeed, how the wings spread, how the soul is borne up to the purest heights, beyond the reach of everything! . . .[13]

In the land where the ancients believed they heard the sirens singing, Nietzsche and Wagner met for the last time, attracted by melodies and passions henceforth radically different. It was probably during these few days when they lived near one another that Wagner confessed to Nietzsche the ecstasies that he experienced when he thought of the Holy Grail and the Eucharist. This was, for Nietzsche, the last straw . . . for the man who, already, had not withstood the disillusionment of the festival at Bayreuth and who, well before, had begun to take the first steps in the direction of *his own* path. The beautiful friendship and the intellectual solidarity, the brotherhood of arms at the heart of the Bayreuth project for the rebirth of Hellenic civilization in Germany thanks to the magic of Wagner's musical theater were extinguished at the Hôtel Vittoria. Without a scandal. Their relations cooled, their paths diverged: everything was clear from then on, and everything was over. The philosopher and the musician would thereafter attack one another publicly—Nietzsche in *Things Human, All Too Human*, Wagner in an article in the *Bayreuther Blätter* titled "Public and Popularity"—but without naming one another explicitly. Only several days after Wagner's death, in February 1883, Nietzsche revealed to Malwida von Meysenbug what he had undergone after the festival of Bayreuth:

Wagner's death shocked me tremendously; and even if I've managed to get out of bed, I am still feeling its aftereffects. —I believe, however, that this event will, in the long term, be a relief for me. It was hard, very hard, to have to be the enemy, for six years, of a person so venerated and adored by everyone, as I loved Wagner; and then, as his enemy, to have to hold my silence out of respect for what the man deserved in his *totality*. Wagner offended me in a *mortal* way—I want you to know it!—His slow and slinking return to Christianity and to the Church, I felt this to be a personal insult against me: my entire youth and its aspirations seemed tarnished by the fact that I had revered a mind capable of taking *this* step. That I should feel this so strongly—is required of me by goals and tasks that I will leave unspoken. *Now*, I regard this step as the step of a Wagner who was growing *old*; it is difficult to die at the right time.[14]

In 1886, in the drafts for the preface of the second edition of *Things Human, All Too Human*, Nietzsche returns again to this incident: "Concerning Richard Wagner, I have not overcome the disillusionment of the summer of 1876: the quantity of imperfections of the work and the man were all at once too great: I fled from them [. . .]. That he, growing old, had changed, this matters little to me: nearly all romantics of this type end up under the cross—I only loved the Wagner that I knew, that is, an honest atheist and immoralist, who invented the character of Siegfried, that of an entirely free man. Since then, he has given sufficiently to understand the extent to which, from the modest corner of his 'Bayreuther Blätter,' he knew how to value the blood of the Redeemer, and—he has been understood. Many Germans, many pure and impure fools of all kinds believe, since then, in Richard Wagner as in their 'Redeemer.' All of this disgusts me."[15] The final version of the preface will speak of Wagner as a desperate romantic who bows down to the Christian cross, conquered by the fanaticism and the hypocrisy of romantic idealism.[16] Nietzsche remained faithful to the atheist and immoralist Wagner, the revolutionary and the disciple of Feuerbach. It is in this intellectual conflict and not in the vicissitudes of a personal relationship that the motivation for his detachment from the maestro is to be found. In Sorrento, however, Nietzsche had not expressed the painful internal change that had occurred in him. Only the manuscripts in which *Things Human, All Too Human* is prepared bear witness to it. And even in the fragments and aphorisms that these pages contain, the reflections on genius, on art, on metaphysics remain rather general and the polemic with Wagner is most often implicit.

From October 27 to November 7, the guests at the Villa Rubinacci and those at the Hôtel Vittoria probably exchanged several visits. Brenner tells us that they went to see the Wagners half a dozen times and we know from Cosima's diary that they went on several outings together. The fact is that Malwida's company was greatly appreciated at the Hôtel Vittoria while, on the other hand, Dr. Rée was not appreciated at all: "*November 1.* In the evening, we are visited by Dr. Rée, whose cold and precise character does not appeal to us; on closer inspection we come to the conclusion that he must be an Israelite."[17] For Cosima and Richard Wagner, this said it all! Apart from Cosima's very brief allusions, the only testimony of these days is to be found among the memories of Malwida von Meysenbug the "idealist":

The first month was graced by the presence of Wagner and his family, who had taken a journey to Italy to recover from the efforts of the summer performances. They were staying in a hotel several paces from us, and I naturally spent a great deal of time with them, mostly with Cosima, whom I loved dearly, for whom I had a high esteem and whose company always granted me the purest intellectual and spiritual pleasures. [. . .] Often our quartet was invited to the Wagners' in the evening. However, I was surprised to notice a constrained cheerfulness and an effort to seem natural in Nietzsche's speech and behavior, which was strange for him. Yet as he was never unpleasant and never turned against the association with the Wagners, I did not suspect that his sympathies could have changed and I threw myself with all my heart into this prolongation of the joys of Bayreuth in a circle of such magnificent people.[18]

The Wagners left for Naples and Nietzsche remained in Sorrento with his friends, at the Villa Rubinacci. Astounded and overwhelmed, he laughed secretly at the maestro's religious postures, as he would later say: "It was a moment when I began, in secret, to laugh at Richard Wagner: at the time when he was preparing to play his final role and appeared before his dear Germans with the gestures of a thaumaturge, a redeemer, a prophet, and even a philosopher. And since I had not yet ceased to love him, my own laughter gnawed at my heart: such is the story of all those who become independent from their masters and at last find their own way."[19] But how to find his own path, how to learn to walk alone, without Schopenhauer and Wagner and, potentially, even against them? Despite the bad condition of his health and his suffering eyes, Nietzsche begins to write again and realizes that the moment has come to make public his subterranean reflections, not only by allusions and fragments, as he had done before in *The Birth of Tragedy* and in the *Untimely Meditations*, but as a whole and in a coherent fashion, developing and completing them with the new ideas that settled day after day on the pages of his notebooks, thanks, in part, to a dialogue with a series of books that he had bought throughout the previous months and which he was reading with Paul Rée and with the little circle of friends at the Villa Rubinacci. These "ideas *regarded as disgraceful*" of which we spoke earlier[20] will thus give him the impulse for his new book, *Things Human, All Too Human*, which, with a dedication to the memory of Voltaire, inaugurates the mature phase of his philosophy.

After the Sorrento days, the two men never saw one another again. Wagner returned home from Italy with the plan to write *Parsifal*. He devoted himself entirely to this work of writing and when the text was finished, sent it to Nietzsche, who, for his part, had just finished the manuscript of *Things Human, All Too Human*. Thus the philosopher describes to us, ten years later, in *Ecce Homo*, this "crossing of two swords":

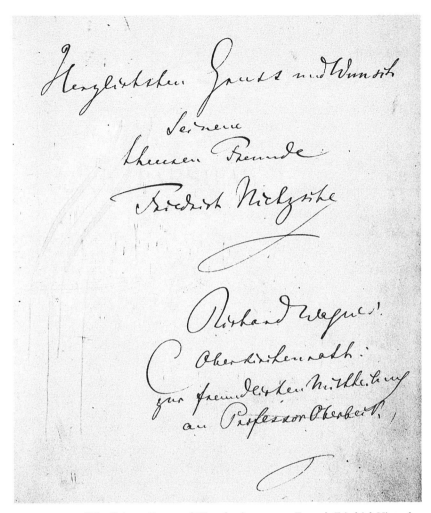

FIGURE 14: "Herzlichsten Gruss und Wunsch seinem teuren Freunde Friedrich Nietzsche. Richard Wagner. Oberkirchenrath: zur freundlichen Mittheilung an Professor Overbeck." Wagner's inscription to Nietzsche on the copy of *Parsifal*. Herzogin Anna Amalia Bibliothek, shelf mark C 522, 3.

When the book was finally finished and in my hands—a profound surprise for one so seriously ill—I also sent two copies, among others, to Bayreuth. By a miraculously meaningful coincidence, I received at the very same time a beautiful copy of the text of *Parsifal*, with Wagner's inscription for me, "for his dear friend, Friedrich Nietzsche, Richard Wagner, Church Councilor."— This crossing of the two books—I felt as if I heard an ominous sound. Did it not seem, rather, like the sound of two *swords* crossing? . . . At any rate, both of us felt that way; for both of us remained silent.— Around that time the first *Bayreuther Blätter* appeared: I understood for *what* it was high time.— Incredible! Wagner had become pious . . .[21]

Wagner's inscription can still be read today on the copy of *Parsifal* that Nietzsche received on January 3, 1878. The first reaction to reading this holy drama (*Bühnenweihfestspeil*) can be found in the letter of the following day to Reinhart von Seydlitz:

Yesterday I received, at my house, *Parsifal*, sent by Wagner. Impressions of the first reading: more Liszt than Wagner, spirit of the counterreformation; for me, too accustomed to the Greek spirit, which represents all that is humanly universal, everything in *Parsifal* is too Christian, too limited in time; the most fantastic psychology; no flesh and much too much blood (the Eucharist in particular is much too bloody for my taste), and then I don't care for hysterical wenches; many things that are bearable to the inner eye will become unbearable in the performance: imagine our actors praying, trembling with their necks twisted. Even the interior of the castle of the Grail *cannot* be effective onstage, as well as the wounded swan. All of these beautiful contrivances belong to the *epos* and, as I said, to the inner eye. The language sounds like a translation into a foreign tongue. But the situations and their sequence—is that not the highest poetry? Is that not the final challenge of music?[22]

Yet in spite of all these aesthetic and philosophical reasons, Nietzsche still regretted the loss of Wagner's friendship and sympathy. One letter to Heinrich Köstelitz is especially explicit:

I, for my part, suffer terribly when I am deprived of sympathy; and, for example, nothing can console me from having lost, in the last few years, Wagner's sympathy. How often I dream of him, and he always appears to me as he was during the time when we were together in confidence! No unkind word has ever been spoken between us, not even in my dreams; on the contrary, we exchanged many encouraging and bright words, and I have perhaps never laughed so much with anyone as with him. All of that is past now—and of what use is it to know that I am *right, against* him on so many matters! That cannot efface the memory of this lost sympathy! I have already experienced something like this and it will probably happen to me again. These are the hardest sacrifices that my course in life and thought have required of me—even now, when I spend an hour in sympathetic conversation with complete strangers, my entire philosophy falters and it seems to me so foolish to want to be right, at the price of love, and not *to be able to communicate* one's most precious gift, in order not to destroy this sympathy. *Hinc meae lacrimae.*[23]

THE MONASTERY OF FREE SPIRITS

After Wagner's departure, life at the Villa Rubinacci became more regularly structured, as Malwida explains:

> Our life in Sorrento organized itself very comfortably. In the morning we were never together; everyone attended to his own occupations in total freedom. The midday meal was the first to reunite us, and sometimes in the afternoon we would take a stroll together through the enchanting surroundings, among the gardens of orange and lemon trees as tall as our apple and pear trees and whose branches, covered in golden fruit, bent over the garden walls and cast their shadows along the path; or we would climb up gently sloping hills and pass by farms where lovely girls were dancing the tarantella—not the contrived tarantella that bands of decked-out ladies dance in hotels for foreigners these days, but the rustic dance full of natural and innocent grace. Often, we would take longer excursions, riding on donkeys, which are reserved there for mountain paths, and our laughter and merriment on those occasions knew no bounds; the young Brenner especially, with his awkward, schoolboyish manner and his long legs that nearly trotted alongside those of the donkey, was the target of many good-natured jokes. In the evening, we reconvened for dinner and then in the sitting room, for animated conversation and communal readings.[24]

In a series of letters to Nietzsche's mother and sister, Paul Rée described the life of the little German colony in Sorrento. Let us read the first letter, written several days after their arrival:

> Dearest Fräulein!
>
> On behalf of your brother, allow me to give you a short report of Southern Italy in general and of Sorrento in particular. As far as Southern Italy in general is concerned, it is just as cold as in Northern Germany, the only difference being that there are no furnaces in the rooms. Sorrento in particular is so beautiful—my room looks onto orange groves, beyond them the blue sea and on the other shore, the hills of Naples—that, if I were a landscape painter, I would

never finish describing it to you today. But since, luckily for you, I am not a painter, I will tell you instead about the greatest curiosity in Sorrento, namely, your brother. At the moment, he is sitting in the only heated room, dictating his fifth *Untimely* to Brenner. He looks good (tanned) and has improved remarkably over the past eight days. [. . .]

Here is the daily timetable. At seven in the morning, your brother drinks milk, a beverage that agrees with him particularly well. Over tea, he dictates something or other until lunchtime, usually. The food is always simple and hearty, thanks to the care of Miss von Meysenbug, that wise lady with the goodness of an angel. After lunch, the great, general siesta, then a communal stroll. Lately, your brother has been capable of walking for hours on end, even on mountain paths, and this is doubtless the main reason why he has been spared headaches since his last seizure, which was brief, but still extremely violent.[25]

Amid this Southern nature and the happy circle of this little community at the Villa Rubinacci,[26] Nietzsche feels lightened and as if reconciled with life: "Our little circle brings together much meditation and friendship, many aspirations and hopes—in short, a great deal of happiness; I feel this in spite of all my pains and in spite of the dire perspectives on my health. Perhaps it is possible to find a little bit more felicity in this world, but in the meantime I wish from the bottom of my heart for all people to have as good a time as we, as I: then they may be satisfied."[27] What the philosopher confided to his Parisian friend he must also have expressed many times to his friends in Sorrento. Malwida, describing these blissful days with her "three sons," as she called them, recounts to us: "Nietzsche said recently that he has never felt so good in his life and that he will probably never feel this good again. Indeed, he is much better, he said, and is beginning to sense what health is."[28]

The daily schedule includes, in the evening, at least two hours of communal reading in the sitting room, by the fireplace. Malwida's letters give us a description of the atmosphere during these evenings shared by the little community in Sorrento: "In the evening, at home once again, Rée reads to us for an hour before dinner and for an hour after dinner. At nine o'clock we go to bed. We are currently reading Voltaire's *Zadig* and *Le siècle de Louis XIV*, by which we are entranced. Nietzsche and Rée especially are fervent admirers of old French literature. You could give me great pleasure if you wanted to send me Diderot's works, at least the masterpieces: *Jean* [probably *Jacques le fataliste*] and *Le neveu de Rameau*."[29] Together, they read the ancients and the moderns, literature as well as philosophy and history: Thucydides and Plato,

FIGURE 15: The Villa Rubinacci in 1927, now the Hotel Eden. From Associazione di studi storici sorrentini, *Sorrento e la sua storia* (Di Mauro: 1991, 159).

Herodotus and the New Testament; Goethe, Mainländer, Spir, Burckhardt, Ranke; Voltaire, Diderot, Charles de Rémusat, Michelet, Daudet; Calderón, Cervantes, Moreto, Lope de Vega; Turgenev, Alexander Herzen's *Memoirs*; the novel *Lorenzo Benoni* by Iacopo Ruffini, etc. At the end of the winter, the assessment is not difficult to draw up for Malwida:

> It is one of the most fascinating winters I've ever spent in my life. I am learning, in my old age, as I would have always liked to learn; Rée, with his readings, is quite simply my benefactor; when I think, now, of my evenings last winter, often so gloomy, when I was alone and had nothing to do, and now every evening, intimately and without *gêne*,[30] in my armchair by the fireplace, the splendid readings, with spirited remarks, often interrupted by hearty laughter—no, truly, I only dread the time when it will end. Ours is a singular, perhaps unprecedented mode of communal living; but it succeeds perfectly, and we form the most peaceful family, as no one could even imagine. So please tell everyone who is worried about it that I am *utterly* happy and that I've never had such a lovely winter.[31]
>
> When we are reunited this way in the evening, Nietzsche sitting comfortably in the armchair behind his eyeglasses, Dr. Rée, our beneficent reader, at the table where the lamp burns, the young Brenner by the fireplace next to me and helping me peel oranges for dinner, I often say, jokingly: "We truly represent an ideal family; four people who, previously, hardly knew each other, who have no relational bond, no common memories, and who now lead a life together in perfect harmony, in untroubled freedom, satisfying both intellectually and with respect to personal comfort."[32]

They also read the French translation of the fourth *Untimely Meditation* and, as a sign of affection, pick flowers in the fields to send them to the translator, a dear friend of Nietzsche's: "Here, dear Madam, are a couple of flowers from the fields of Sorrento. We all wish to express to you our esteem and admiration, for we have read your book over the past few evenings with ever-renewed astonishment. Brenner picked these flowers along the rocks of the shore, Miss von Meysenbug arranged them."[33] But mostly on those Sorrentino evenings, they read the notes taken by a pupil of Nietzsche's during the course on Greek civilization by the famous historian of Basel: Jacob Burckhardt.

> We had with us a rich and excellent selection of books, but the most beautiful of this variety was a manuscript of notes from Jacob Burckhardt's lectures on Greek culture held at the University of Basel, taken by a pupil of Nietzsche's

and brought along on the journey. Nietzsche gave an oral commentary on it and surely there has never been anywhere else a more marvelous and accomplished presentation of this most beautiful cultural era of humanity, in both writing and speech, through these two greatest experts on Greek antiquity. My predilection for this glorious golden age of the human spirit then gained its highest exaltation. I was thus enraptured by Burckhardt's definition of the being of the Greek people: "Pessimism of the worldview and optimism of the temperament." Certainly a splendid alloy to create a perfect people.[34]

The pupil of Nietzsche's was Louis Kelterborn and his notebook is still conserved today in Nietzsche's library at Weimar. On page eighty-three, we can read: "The religion and reflection were pessimistic, but the temperament was optimistic; hence an enormous productivity [. . .] The people was full of elastic forces, hence its lively and optimistic temperament, which constantly drove it to new actions. But its vision of life was entirely pessimistic."[35] "Pessimism of the intelligence and optimism of the will": this formula, which still appears often among intellectuals as well as French and Italian leftist political parties, is usually attributed to Antonio Gramsci, who practically considered it his motto and had taken it from Romain Rolland. What was unknown, however, until Mazzino Montinari brought it to light in 1973, is that Romain Rolland had very likely read it in the passage: "Pessimism of the worldview and optimism of the temperament," which we have just quoted from Nietzsche's friend Malwida. The origin of the famous formula used by Gramsci is therefore to be found in the oral commentary that Nietzsche had given of Burckhardt's text during the evenings of reading in Sorrento, by the fireplace in the sitting room of the Villa Rubinacci.[36]

On the model of their little community's happy and instructive life, the guests at the Villa Rubinacci daydreamed about reuniting teachers and friends around the project of a school designed to educate the educators. It was a question of an idea dear to Nietzsche: "*To educate the educators! But they must educate themselves!* It is for them that I write." To realize this dream, Nietzsche desired to summon up extremely various skills: "*School of Educators.* Where is / the doctor / the naturalist / the economist / the cultural historian / the expert on the history of the Church / the expert on the Greeks / the expert on the State." Before leaving for Italy, he had written to his new friend, Reinhardt von Seydlitz, trying to attract him to Sorrento: "Why am I telling you all this? Oh, you can guess my secret hope: we are staying in Sorrento for almost a year. Then I will return to Basel, unless I establish my monastery somewhere, in the *great* style, I mean the 'school of educators' (where they educate *themselves*)."[37]

In the "Sorrento papers," this idea is reaffirmed and juxtaposed with the image of the free spirit:

> The *school* of *educators* is founded on the basis of this insight: that our edu-cators are not themselves educated, that the need for this is ever greater but the quality is ever poorer, that the sciences, given the natural fragmentation of fields of activity, cannot prevent individual barbarism, that there is no tribunal of civilization that considers the intellectual prosperity of humankind without taking account of national interests: an international department of education.[38]
>
> He who wishes to use his money as a free spirit should found institutes on the model of monasteries, to make it possible for people who want nothing more to do with the world to live a communal life amicably and in the greatest simplicity.[39]

Malwida had a slightly more sentimental, but also more practical, vision of the matter and was already thinking of premises in which to begin the new school:

> I received, at that time, a great many letters from women and young girls of all classes who, after reading my *Memoirs of an Idealist*, expressed their sympathy to me, which continued to happen in the following years, to my greatest joy and satisfaction. This circumstance nourished an idea that had already occurred to me and which I had communicated to my companions, namely, to found a kind of mission house to lead adults of both sexes toward the free development of the noblest intellectual life, so that they could then go back out into the world and spread the seeds of a new and spiritual culture. The idea found the most fervent approval among the gentlemen; Nietzsche and Rée were both equally prepared to participate as teachers. I was convinced that I would be able to draw many female students here because I wanted to devote a particular effort to training them as the noblest advocates of the emancipation of women so that they could help to preserve this most important cultural work, full of significance, from misunderstanding and disfigurement and guide it in a purer, more dignified direction, to a more beneficent development. We were already looking for a proper venue, because the school was to open in magnificent Sorrento, in bliss-ful nature and not in urban narrowness. On the beach, we had found several spacious grottoes, like great rooms inside of rocks, which had clearly been ex-panded by human labor: there was even a kind of platform that seemed to be explicitly intended for a lecturer. We thought that they were perfectly appro-priate to hold our lectures in on hot summer days. And in general, all of the

FIGURE 16: The Capucin monastery, the building chosen for the school of educators, now the Grand Hôtel Cocumella. From Fiorentino, 160 (photo Esposito).

teaching had to be conceived as a reciprocal learning process after the manner of the peripatetics, and more on the model of the Greeks than the moderns.[40]

Reinhart von Seydlitz, who had finally come to Sorrento, saw the school of educators already realized by the little community of guests at the Villa Rubinacci:

[Malwida] ruled like a venerable abbess in the "monastery of free spirits," which at that time, for lack of a better place, had its domicile in the Villa Rubinacci, a hotel in the town. What plans were forged under the mild sun, amid the gentle roar of the purple-blue sea [. . .]! We already had our eye on the local, disestablished, and abandoned Capuchin monastery with a view to transforming it into a "school for educators" where "they educate themselves," and—that's how practical we were!—to furnish one half of it as a hotel for foreigners with all the paraphernalia, so that *this* half could provide the necessary financial basis for the *other*, idealistic one.[41]

Carried away by his enthusiasm, Nietzsche practically believes in it and engages his sister: "The 'school of educators' (also called modern monastery, ideal colony, *université libre*) is in the air, who knows what will happen! In our mind's eye, we have already appointed you to direct all the administration of our institute of forty people. You must, above all, learn Italian!"[42] The Capuchin monastery will remain the ideal site for the school of educators until the end of the stay, which will also mark the end of the project.

DREAMING OF THE DEAD

After two months of life in Sorrento, what assessment can Nietzsche draw up of his health in December 1876? From a strictly physical point of view, his situation has hardly improved: he can neither read nor write and feels idle like a tourist, or like a philosopher. He thus gives himself over to the company of his friends and, especially, he reflects, dreams, revisits his past life.

> Dear, faithful friend, after a glimmer of recovery, I have been so ill again, so unceasingly ill, that I no longer dare to hope. The external conditions for regaining health are, however, all present and something *must* come of that, mustn't it? But patience is necessary (Nietzsche to Overbeck, December 6, 1876).

> Several horrible days that nearly made me desperate. Now things are going a bit better again. The weather is very mild, yesterday Rée went for a swim in the sea. I am taking a lot of walks, digestion and sleep still very good (to his family, December 7, 1876).

> I take a great many walks. Have entirely abandoned all work, even dictation and discussion. What will come of it! (to his family, December 15, 1876).

> Sorrento seems to be made for recovery. I have become much stronger; not a single stomach problem yet. But every week, a day of severe headaches: that has not changed (to his family, December 24, 1876).

> Even here, my health doesn't want to improve, pains, pains! If I could abstract from it, my situation here would make the gods envious. Rée has just finished writing a book, Brenner is writing novellas, Miss von Meysenbug a novel, and I am read to, because I haven't the right either to read or to write (to Rohde, December 30, 1876).[43]

And yet, on December 19, 1876, Nietzsche took it upon himself to write a long and important letter to Cosima Wagner on her birthday.[44] This letter reads as a kind of assessment, no longer of his state of health but of his state of mind, as if it were a way of slowly taking leave of a phase in his life. Between the memory of the previous stages and the premonition, still hazy, of the coming evolution, many sensitive points of the young philosopher's relationship with Richard Wagner are indirectly and accidentally evoked in a manner that presages, after the chilling-over of their relations, a new development of this restless spirit.

Dearest Lady!

Your birthday is here and I know no word with which I can think to express your feelings at this moment. Wishes? You wish for happiness?— I hardly understand these words any longer when I think of you; when one has learned to take life greatly, the difference between happiness and unhappiness falls away and one goes beyond "wishes." All that your life depends on should happen exactly as it has happened and, in particular, it is impossible to imagine the whole after-Bayreuth any differently than it is presently: it corresponds perfectly to the whole before-Bayreuth; what was sordid and desolate then still is now, and what was great has remained so, or rather, it is now with all the more reason. We can only *celebrate* such days as yours, and not wish you happiness. One grows quieter from year to year and in the end, one no longer says anything serious about personal matters.

The distance of my current way of life, which illness has imposed upon me, is so great that the past eight years have left my mind and the earlier times of my life, of which I hadn't thought amid the endless hardships of these years, are forced upon me violently. Nearly every night, in my dreams, I am in the company of long-forgotten people, above all with the dead. The times of childhood, boyhood, and school are all very present to me; contemplating the goals that I had set for myself earlier and what I actually achieved, I am struck by the fact that I went far beyond the general hopes and wishes of youth; and in contrast, I have still succeeded in accomplishing only a third of what I had seriously resolved to do. Things will probably remain as they are in the future. If I were completely healthy—who knows if I would not set adventurous tasks for myself? Unfortunately, I am obliged to lower my sails a bit. For the coming years at Basel, I have resolved to bring several philological works to completion, and my friend Köselitz has declared himself willing to help me as a secretary, reading to me and writing for me (since my eyes are as good as gone). Once the *Philologica* are in order, something more difficult awaits me: will you be surprised if I confess to you a divergence from Schopenhauer's doctrine that has emerged gradually and of which I became aware almost unexpectedly? I disagree with him on nearly all of his general principles; already, when I wrote about Schopenhauer, I realized that I had overcome everything dogmatic in him; for me, the *man* was everything. In the meantime, my "reason" has been very active—because of this, life has become a bit harder and the burden greater! How can one bear it until the end!

Do you know that my teacher Ritschl has died? I received the news almost together with the messages announcing the death of my grandmother and of Gerlach, my philologist colleague at Basel. Even this year, a letter from

Ritschl had reawakened in me the touching impression that I had retained from his earlier relations with me: he confirmed his affectionate confidence and faithfulness to me, even if he regarded as inevitable a temporary difficulty in our relationship, a respectful separation. I owe to him the single, essential benefit of my life, my position as professor of philology at Basel: I owe it to his freedom of thought, his sharpness of eye, and his generosity toward young people. [. . .]

> In faithful adoration,
> your Friedrich Nietzsche
> Sorrento, Villa Rubinacci
> I forgot the respects of Dr. Rée.

The first thing that strikes us about a man suspended between past and future is the dreams in which Nietzsche is visited by people from the past or from beyond the grave. This motif reappears nearly two years later among short notations in a little notebook titled *Memorabilia*. This time, it is accompanied by another significant image: "In Sorrento, I lifted the moss layer of nine years. Dreaming of the dead."[45] Let us analyze these two motifs, beginning with the first. The image of the layer of moss is also present in three letters written on August 28, 1877 from Rosenlauibad, where Nietzsche ended his sabbatical year in the forest of the Swiss mountains:

> Now my thoughts push me forward, I have such a rich year behind me (in inner results); it seems to me as if it had been enough to lift up the old moss layer of daily, necessary philological work—and underneath it, everything is green and lush. I think with frustration that I must leave all the benefits of my work behind now and perhaps lose the fresh feelings and everything else with them! If only I had a cottage somewhere. Then I could take walks every day for six to eight hours as I do here, and I would think between me and myself of what I would later jot down on paper at home, swiftly and with perfect certainty—I did this in Sorrento, I do this here, and in this way I have gotten *a lot* out of an altogether unpleasant and clouded year.[46]
>
> What shall I tell you of myself? How every morning, already two hours before the sun comes up in the mountains, I am on the road and still in the long shadows of the afternoon and evening? How I have thought through many things and felt so rich after this year, which has finally allowed me to take off the old moss layer of the daily *constraint* of teaching and thinking?[47]

How much I have devised! How rich I feel! And now everything will have to be buried once more under a moss layer! Absolutely nauseating![48]

The meaning of the appearance of the dead in dreams is explained and expanded in aphorism 360 of *Assorted Opinions and Maxims*, the small volume that Nietzsche published in 1879 and which represents a kind of appendix to *Things Human, All Too Human*:

> *Indication of great changes.* —If we dream of people we have long since forgotten or who have for long been dead, it is a sign that we have gone through a great change within ourselves and that the ground upon which we live has been completely turned over [*umgegraben*]: so that the dead rise up and our antiquity [*Alterthum*] becomes our modernity [*Neuthum*].[49]

The profound change that Nietzsche is in the process of living, as we have seen, is the distancing of his recent past: the Basel years, the friendship with Wagner, and the whole constellation of ideas of *The Birth of Tragedy* and of the *Untimely Meditations* seem to him, now, to be very far away. This change digs deep into his soul and produces something like a reversal: it exhumes earlier states of mind and buries those that are recent (*umgraben*). It is not by chance that the first notations that Nietzsche had written during the summer of 1876, the first kernel of the thoughts of *Things Human, All Too Human*, was titled *Die Pflugschar*, "The Plowshare," a technical term designating the piece of iron in the plow that serves to chop and turn over clumps of earth. Following this reversal, ancient things become new again and vice versa. Nietzsche constructs a couple of terms of which the first, *Alterthum*, is of common usage while the second, *Neuthum*, is a very rare term in the German language. In Nietzsche's works, it appears only twice. The first time was in the third paragraph of the *Untimely* on history (1874). Nietzsche wrote, therein, that antiquarian history venerates the past so much that it does not dare replace it with the present; that it does not dare replace antiquity (*Alterthum*) with novelty (*Neuthum*).[50] In the aphorism of *Assorted Opinions and Maxims*, on the contrary, the habits of the past are not sterilely venerated, but are resuscitated and become themselves the new present: the dead are resuscitated in the same moment as the present is buried. In Sorrento, memories, impressions, aspirations of his childhood and his adolescence surface in his consciousness and visit his dreams. But mostly, intellectual experiences, his first moments of contact with philosophy are what come back into his mind. He became a professor at the age of twenty-four, thus going, indeed, "far beyond the general hopes and wishes of youth," but he is now conscious of the fact that he never succeeded in developing what truly interested him. Nine years earlier, from October 1867 to March 1868, when he was doing his military service as an artilleryman on horseback, he had begun a whole series of philosophical studies on teleology, "on the concept of the organic, from Kant to our time," and on the materialism of the ancients and the moderns. At the end of his university studies and before becoming a professor, the young Hellenist had thus felt arise in him a gradual passage from philology to the materialist philosophy of his age surrounding the figure of Democritus, "the only philosopher who still lives."[51] His appointment at Basel, which came about at this exact time, had forced him to abandon everything. Between Basel and Wagner's residence in Tribschen, he had been swept up in the Wagnerian fervor and had given birth to a strange "centaur"—as he himself called it—a book on the birth of tragedy out of the spirit of music, which had brought him a certain amount of notoriety, a very close relationship with the maestro, but also the incomprehension of his colleagues. Of course, even in this period of work and battle, his reflections on the ancient philosophers had maintained a decisive place in his mind, as his courses on "The pre-Platonic philosophers" demonstrate, but they were as if buried under the "moss layer" of his philological work and under the radiance of his public activity in favor of the Wagnerian cause.

In short, if Cosima was willing to read this letter, it said to her, first: "I wanted to be a philosopher and not a professor of philology, not a Wagnerian propagandist." Then it expressed Nietzsche's intention to resume, first, his philological-philosophical work on Democritus in order to take on, afterwards, "something more difficult": a critique of Schopenhauer's philosophy. We know from his notebooks that much earlier, at the time of his military service, he had written a detailed refutation of Schopenhauer's philosophy: twenty hard, pitiless pages that began with the observation that the Schopenhauerian attempt to explain the enigma of the world on the basis of the notion of "Will" had failed.[52] In 1878, he will make a distinction between his own position and the effect that Schopenhauer's metaphysics was producing on the elite class of the era. The elites, he claimed, used Schopenhauer's metaphysics as a kind of introduction to religion: "Everyone becomes *pious* and pushes aside the corporeal Schopenhauer, of a Voltairian mind, for whom his fourth book would be incomprehensible. My mistrust of the system *from the beginning*. The *person* came to the fore, the *type* of the philosopher and catalyst of civilization. The *general worship*, for its part, drew on the ephemeral aspects of his doctrine, on what had *not* left its mark on his life—in contrast to me. The creation of the philosopher was the only thing of value and consequence *for me*—but *I* was inhibited by the superstition of *genius*. Close your eyes."[53]

Nietzsche's philosophy has traditionally been divided into three phases, of which the first would include *The Birth of Tragedy* and the *Untimely Meditations*, the second the three great books of aphorisms—*Things Human, All Too Human, Daybreak,* and *The Gay Science*—and of which the last would cover the *Zarathustra* period until the end of Nietzsche's conscious life. This tripartition, which serves essentially to marginalize the period of the free spirit, to minimize the importance of the supposedly "positivist" phase, and to instate a continuity between the first and the third phases, between *The Birth of Tragedy* and *Zarathustra,* for example, or between the Nietzschean will to power and the Schopenhauerian will to live, is untenable.[54] Nietzsche himself underlines here the continuity between his first philosophical reflections contained in the journals of his youth and the philosophy of the free spirit of *Things Human, All Too Human*. It is thus the Wagnerian period that is, in truth, only a clearly distinct *phase* in the evolution of Nietzsche's philosophy. The proof of this, moreover, is that even at the height of the Wagnerian phase, there remain, in Nietzsche's texts, hesitations and strong ambiguities with regard to the Wagnerian project of a mythical foundation of German culture, which Nietzsche had interpreted in *The Birth of Tragedy*. This is most evident in his reflections on the pre-Platonic philosophers, which are realized in the form of a series of university courses and an essay on *Philosophy in the Tragic Age of the Greeks* and which amount, within the Wagnerian phase itself, to an unresolved tension between the mythical, cohesive strength of art and the analytical and disintegrating spirit of philosophy. It would thus be necessary to put the Wagnerian phase between parentheses and establish a stronger continuity between the first reflections of the early writings and the philosophy of the free spirit contained in *Things Human, All Too Human*.

We would then see that Nietzsche's philosophy does not begin with the metaphysics of art of *The Birth of Tragedy*, under Schopenhauer's aegis and on Wagner's side, but with the praise of Democritus, the draft of an essay against teleology and a pitiless critique of Schopenhauer's metaphysics.

Cosima was very troubled by this evolution: the name of Schopenhauer was one of the strong points of Nietzsche and Wagner's friendship. In her long response, she asks of him first: "I would very much like to know more about your divergence from Schopenhauer," and further on she insists: "It would truly enthrall me to know your objections against our philosopher. Wouldn't you like to dictate a letter to Brenner?"[55] In her diaries, we read: "Nice letter from Prof. Nietzsche, though informing us that he now rejects Schopenhauer's

FIGURE 17: Friedrich Nietzsche in 1873. GSA 101/15.

teachings! . . ."[56] Cosima would have been even more troubled if she had known what was brewing in the Sorrento papers that Nietzsche kept secret for the time being, but to which he was alluding when he spoke of the exercise of his reason: "In the meantime, my 'reason' has been very active—because of this, life has become a bit harder and the burden greater!" Cosima had, however, understood that something new and alarming was happening to her friend. She wrote to Malwida, several weeks later:

> I think that there is in Nietzsche a darkly creative substratum of which he is himself hardly conscious; it is from this that the important element in him springs, but he takes alarm at it; whereas all that he says and thinks, however luminous (*lichterhellt*) it may be, is really not worth much. In him it is the tellurian element that is of importance, while the solar element is insignificant and even worrying and uninvigorating to him, owing to the conflict with the tellurian. [. . .] "Great thoughts come from the heart," says Vauvenargues, a dictum which may be applied to Nietzsche, for his great thoughts come to him, not from his brain, but from what? Ah, who can say?[57]

In the chapter of *Zarathustra* dedicated to the isle of tombs, where the visions and apparitions of youth are buried, strangled too soon by Zarathustra's enemies, we find a name for that obscure force that nothing could ever bury and that guides the soul through its passings:

> How did I endure it? How did I surmount and overcome such wounds? How did my soul rise again from such tombs?
>
> Indeed, in me there is something invulnerable and unburiable, something that explodes rock: that is *my will*. Silent and unchanged it strides through the years. It would walk its way on my feet, my old will, and its mind is hard of heart and invulnerable.
>
> Invulnerable am I only in the heel. You are still alive and your old self, most patient one. You have still broken out of every tomb. What in my youth was unredeemed lives on in you; and as life and youth you sit there, full of hope, on yellow ruins of tombs.
>
> Indeed, for me, you are still the shatterer of all tombs. Hail to tell, my will! And only where there are tombs are there resurrections.[58]

Alongside this force, which guides the evolution of his mind, another figure and another spirit dominate Nietzsche's letter, that of his "venerated master," the great philologist Friedrich Ritschl. The fact that in the letter to Cosima,

Nietzsche evokes at once the "affectionate confidence" that his master nourished for him and the "temporary difficulty" in their friendship does not come without a supplementary effect of separation and criticism with respect to Wagner. And Cosima hastens to respond on this point: "I understand very well that the death of your teacher affected you deeply; gifted youth clings to the teacher with much love, believing that knowledge is life and holding the man who gives him this knowledge warmly to be an incarnation of God."[59] In reality, as Cosima was well aware, Ritschl had never appreciated the passion with which Nietzsche had thrust himself into the Wagnerian cause. Indeed, the assumption of a mythical, metaphysical, and antihistorical position that had characterized Nietzsche's "Wagnerian works" had been the cause of the tension in their relationship. At Nietzsche's request, the old professor had responded to him on the subject of *The Birth of Tragedy* in 1872:

> I belong, in my entire nature, [. . .] to the *historical* tendency and to the historical consideration of human things with such resolution that the redemption of the world has never seemed to me to be found in one or another of the philosophical systems; that I can never define the natural fading of an era or a phenomenon as "suicide"; that in the individualization of life I cannot recognize a regression, nor believe that the forms and potencies of the intellectual life of a people naturally gifted through their historical development and to a certain extent privileged would be the absolute criteria for all peoples and all times—as little as a *single* religion suffices, has sufficed, will ever suffice the diverse individualities of peoples.— You cannot expect an "Alexandrian" and a scholar to condemn *knowledge* and to see *only* in art the creative, redemptive, and liberating force of the world.[60]

That being said, the old professor had conserved his affection and his confidence in Nietzsche, as we see in the last letter that Nietzsche had received from him, on January 14, 1876, and to which he had alluded in the letter to Cosima: "To your good wishes and faithful sentiments correspond, in heartfelt sincerity, mine and ours. Let the coming year take place with this same inner disposition—in common, if possible!— [. . .] *Vale faveque* T.T. F.R."[61] Remembering this letter, but surely also the other one that we quoted previously, Nietzsche wrote to the widow, Sophie Ritschl, in response to the death notice that he had received on November 17:

> How often, since the sad news, the figure of my dear, great teacher has appeared to me, how often I have passed, in my mind, through the long-gone

FIGURE 18: Friedrich Ritschl. From Alfred Gudemann, *Imagines Philologorum* (Leipzig, 1911).

times, when I was together with him nearly every day, and I have contemplated the countless evidences of his benevolent and truly generous disposition. I am happy to possess a letter from just last year, a precious testimony of his constant charity and affection toward me and to be certain that even where he could not agree with me, he granted me his full confidence. I believed that he would see the day when I would be able to thank him publicly and honor him, as my heart desired to do for so long and in a form that would, perhaps, have pleased him too. Today I mourn over his grave and, owing to my ill health, I must even defer my homage of his memory to an indeterminate future.[62]

What was the form in which Nietzsche wished pay public tribute to his master of philological and historical knowledge? We do not know, but when we see that in the first aphorism of *Things Human, All Too Human*, historical philosophy is posed against metaphysical philosophy, and when in the second, we read that "The lack of a historical sense is the original sin of all philosophers" and that "historical philosophizing is necessary from now on, and with it the virtue of modesty," we think that the master would not have been displeased with his student.

CHAPTER THREE

Walks on the Land of the Sirens

If we wanted to indicate the places in which the philosopher Nietzsche felt at home, we would name: Genoa, Nice, Sils Maria, perhaps Venice, not Basel, absolutely not Naumburg, nor Bonn, nor Leipzig. But if we wanted to relate a period in his life when he took a truly *touristic* journey: there would only be Sorrento. The stay in Sorrento is indeed truly the only one during which Nietzsche enjoyed the spiritual state particular to the traveler, to the man who does not desire to be at home but wants to be elsewhere, who appreciates travel, landscape, the beauties of nature and art with the eyes of a tourist, even if, in Nietzsche's case, the philosopher's gaze often transfigures the places he visits. With the small group of his friends, Nietzsche visits the most evocative locations on the Sorrentino peninsula: Castellammare di Stabia, Vico Equense, Meta, Massa Lubrense, Sant'Agata sui Due Golfi, as well as Naples, Pompeii, and Capri. But mostly he walks on foot, nearly every day, in the hills, on the little beaches, in the forests of orange and olive trees. Here are several excerpts from letters that convey the impressions of the small daily outings:

> Dear friend Köselitz, my best wishes, the day is blue and warm, and in the afternoon we want to take a boat and sail past all the beautiful grottoes that we can along the coast.[1]

> Last week, Nietzsche and I went for a three-hour hike every morning, and, indeed, nothing less than to the Gulf of Salerno, going over the mountains behind Sorrento. The landscape there is entirely different: the sun shines, the

FIGURE 19 : Funeral procession in Naples. Photo Giorgio Sommer.

sea is bluer, the air is balmier, the houses are white and red in the Moorish style, the people are like Egyptians and "butterflies flutter in the sunbeams."[2]

I truly received beautiful New Year's letters on New Year's Day, when I returned from an outing in the country, which we took all together and which lasted the entire day, with glorious weather and an enchanting view of the gulf; we went to one of the royal castles.[3]

But now let us follow the quartet on two particularly important day trips, to Naples and to Capri.

THE CARNIVAL OF NAPLES

In mid-February, when Nietzsche wants to see a renowned German eye doctor from the university for a medical appointment, the friends go to Naples and take advantage of the situation to see the museum, run errands, and attend the carnival.

Malwida relates this to her daughter:

And so we left together, Nietzsche, Trina, and I. Yesterday, Rée and Brenner went before us; Nietzsche was unwell and didn't think he would be able to come. This morning, however, he was feeling better and since he wanted to consult a doctor, we began our trip. The sky was gloomy, but finally brightened. When we arrived, Rée and Brenner were out, so we took a car and left for Toledo, with our iron mask, in the midst of the crowd. God, what we were pelted with! A hail of *coriandoli*, such that we were completely white in an instant and the car was heaped with it. The traffic was dazzling, there were beautiful floats with masks, much more beautiful than in Rome. Nietzsche amused himself a great deal, to my astonishment.[4]

Amid the carnival, in a side street, a funeral car advances slowly, with its mournful weight and its mournful escort. Notebook in hand, the philosopher sets the contrast *and* the similarity between the parade of confetti-covered masks and that of the bereaved murmuring prayers: "A funeral procession in a carnival will someday be historical in the manner that the other floats are, now."[5] Later, when he transcribes this first notation made in a Naples street, he will transfigure the image which, placed into a historical perspective, takes on the meaning of the progressive liberation of humanity in the face of the somber Catholic ritual: carnival of history, funeral procession of the liturgy.

Just as old religious ceremonies that were once meaningful end up as superstitious, misunderstood procedures, so history in general, if it lives on only by way of habit, will seem like magical nonsense or a carnivalesque disguise. The sun, which should illuminate the pope upon the proclamation of infallibility, the dove, which should fly by at that moment, now seem to us like dubious stunts whose only purpose is to deceive; but old civilization is full of them, and doesn't at all distinguish where the deception begins.

In Naples recently, a sumptuous Catholic funeral car moved forward with its procession in one of the side streets while, in immediate proximity, the carnival raged: all of the colorful floats imitated the costume and pomp of past civilizations. But this funeral procession will also someday be such a historical carnival parade; the colorful shell remains and delights but the kernel has escaped, or a fraudulent scheme is hidden there, like the devices that priests use to awaken faith.[6]

After the consultation with Dr. Schrön, the outing in Naples ends with a trip to the museum. Malwida reports:

Nietzsche took great joy in seeing these magnificent things and said that there is nowhere in the world where one can study *Greek* antiquity like this museum.

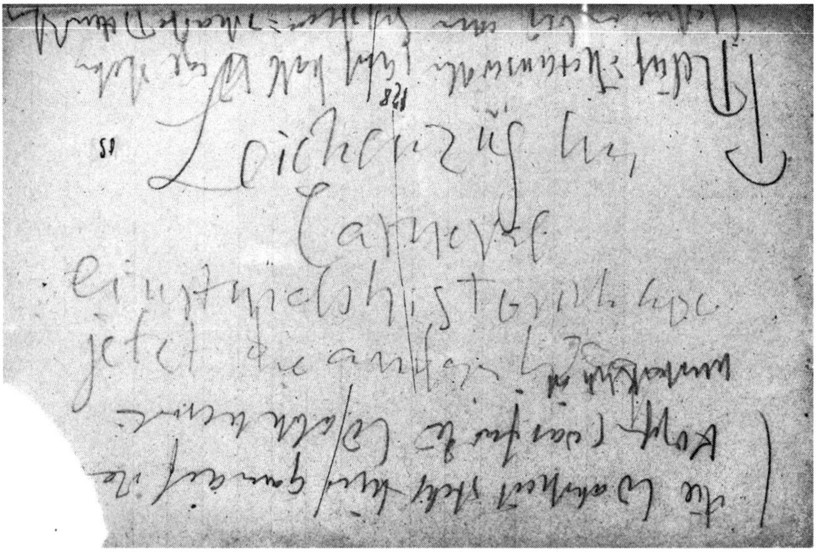

FIGURE 20: *"Leichenzug in Carneval,"* Nietzsche, notebook N II 3, page 47. GSA 71/175.

For Southern Italy was full of Greek colonies and was called Great-Greece, and Pompeii and Herculaneum are full of the traces of Greek culture. Afterwards, we went down to the sea, to S. Lucia, and ate fresh oysters with *Asti Spumante* on them in the open air. [. . .] Then we drove through Posillipo and saw the magnificent light of the sunset on the gulf, the mountains, and the city. Nietzsche said that the only pertinent music that he could think of for such an image was the Benedictus of Beethoven's Great Mass. [. . .] The journey home was terribly painful for Nietzsche and today he is still completely shattered and melancholy, because the doctor gave him two alternatives: either the illness ceases immediately or there could be a nearly total weakening of cerebral activity. His eyes have already gotten so much worse that his future as a philologist seems almost certainly impossible.[7]

MITHRAS AT CAPRI

After a trip to Pompeii in early March, on the morning of the 22nd, the four friends take a boat to Capri. Malwida writes to her daughter:

Yesterday morning, in the beautiful weather, we left Sorrento by the *vapore*, which runs daily as long as the weather is good. At first, when the boat began to sway a bit, Nietzsche felt ill and went to lie down in the cabin, while Rée and I remained on the deck talking, to my great delight (Brenner didn't come with us, he didn't want to). The boat first stopped at the blue grotto, where dinghies wait for foreigners, to take them on tours of it. We too climbed into a dinghy to go inside, but the sea was agitated and when the dinghy came through the narrow opening, an entire wave came over us so that we were completely soaked, a rather unpleasant situation, as you can imagine. There was a multitude of dinghies in the grotto, and cries came from every direction, followed by echoes. We left rather quickly and the enjoyment was consequently ruined. In Capri, we found that all of the hotels were full. Only one, which was new and rather high up, could offer us three rooms. After lunch,[8] we rode donkeys to Salto Tiberio. It was magnificent up there! Oh, how much I have thought of our dinners and the joyful hours we spent there! Our host's widow is still there, the old Corsican is dead, and the little priest, their only son, is now canon of Sorrento. We drank excellent wine from Capri at their hotel and put our signatures in the guest book: "Donna Malwida Cosmopolita; Don Paolo (Rée) *idem*; Don Federigo, *uomo dell'avvenire*!" Then we climbed up to see the hermit, who has held the position for seventeen years. He told me that in January he made a pilgrimage to Rome to see the Pope. The view from there of the two beautiful gulfs was exquisite. Pretty girls danced the tarantella for us. We came back down for dinner and then Nietzsche, who, luckily, found a piano, played very beautifully for us. But unfortunately the weather took a turn for the worse and there was pouring rain and a storm. The night was terrible: I hardly slept at all and had a headache, as did Nietzsche. This morning, we had no idea what to do. The sea was rough, the *vapore* didn't arrive, and it was no use thinking of a little boat. Eventually, the sky cleared and we left for Anacapri, by the beautiful new road that they have made, since the ancient steps no longer exist. There are two cars here now. It was sublime up there; we had lunch, saw charming young girls, and then went to the cemetery, where I visited the grave of the good Sophie Rommel, which is touching and poetic. Then we rested and decided to spend the night in Capri, since the sea was too rough. Then we went to the *arco naturale*, which perhaps you remember. The gentlemen were all delighted. Oh, it really is too beautiful there and it still hasn't yet reached its full beauty, for the vines are not yet green and the sky and sea are not pure blue. We would have loved to take a moonlight walk on the island today, but it is cold out and the moon has not been fully revealed. If the beautiful flowers that we picked in the fields are still fresh when we arrive back in Sorrento, I will send you some. Hopefully, we will return tomorrow, and I will put this letter in the mail straightaway.[9]

From this stay, Malwida will remember, in addition to the beauty of the landscape, the delight that the evening when Nietzsche improvised on the piano brought her: "The winter when I was with him in Sorrento, we went with Dr. Rée for two days to the magical island, at a time when it had not yet been totally corrupted by tourism. One evening, Nietzsche played truly magnificently, mostly improvising; ecstatic at all of the beautiful things we had seen during the day, he was particularly moved and elicited marvelous melodies from his instrument."[10]

Unlike Malwida, Nietzsche hardly mentions this outing to Capri at all in his letters. On March 26, he writes laconically to his mother: "We went to Capri, without much luck; I was ill one day, as on all short journeys."[11] But there is a place in Capri that must have vividly struck his memory: the *"grotta del Matrimonio,"* also called *"grotta di Matromania"* or *"Mitromania."* Malwida's long account does not tell us if, on this night of March 23rd, 1877, the three friends visited this grotto, but it was located just along the path that they took, near the *arco naturale.* About one year later, during the summer of 1878, Nietzsche writes in one of his extremely rare notebooks that contain autobiographical notations, these pithy and enigmatic phrases, under the title, *Memorabilia*:

> *Mitromania.* —Waiting for the appearance of the first sunbeam—*finally* seeing it—ridiculing it and extinguishing *oneself.*
> Mithras—hope
> Mithras madness!
> Grotta di *Matrimonio*, idyllic image of unconscious life.
> To imagine life as a *celebration* beginning with mitromania.
> Art of memory, conquest of evil, bitter elements. Fight against illness vexation boredom.
> 2. Mithras kills the bull, to which the snake and the scorpion cling.[12]

The experience of this trip to Capri was thus filtered through his philosophical sensibility and his classical culture to become the symbol of a profound affirmation of earthly existence. In these lines, Nietzsche is probably also remembering the description that Ferdinand Gregorovius, an old friend of Malwida's, had given of Capri and of the grotto of Matromania in his book of memoirs about his travels in Italy, which served at that time as a travel guide that can still be found in the bookshops of Capri:

> Here, a steep stairway leads down to the middle of the shore, where a deep and beautiful grotto opens up: the enigmatic grotto of Matromania. It is approximately fifty-five feet wide and one hundred feet deep, a work of nature expanded

FIGURE 21: The Grotto of Matromania. Private collection.

by the hand of man; already at the entrance one can see Roman ruins and in the interior, masonry hangs on the walls. In the depths of the grotto, two constructions that look like seats rise up in the form of a semi-circle, facing one another; in between them, there are steps that probably once led to the altar of the god, whose statues were erected there. Everything indicates that this is the cell of a temple. The name Matromania, which the grotto carries and which the people, in unconscious irony, have distorted into Matrimonio [Marriage], as if Tiberius had consummated his marriage here, is derived from *Magnae matris antrum* or from *Magnum Mithrae antrum*. It is said that this sanctuary was dedicated to Mithras, not so much because the Persian god of the sun was honored in the grotto, but because one of the many mural reliefs representing mystical sacrifices to Mithras, of which there are so many in the Vatican museum, was found engraved there. In the *Studi* of Naples, I saw two of these representations: one of the reliefs was found in the grotto of Posillipo, the other in the grotto of Matromania. They show Mithras in Persian garb, kneeling on a bull and plunging the sacrificial knife into its throat, while the snake, the scorpion, and the dog wound the bull.

This grotto of Capri was indeed appropriate for the mystical worship of the sun, for it faces toward the East, and he who, from the depths of the grotto, watches Helios rise and contemplates the purple glow of the mountains and the sea, he truly becomes a worshipper of the sun.[13]

This place marked by mystery was probably home to the ceremonies of a religion of the sun, which, exported from the orient by Roman soldiers and spread throughout the empire between the first and third centuries, led a fierce

F I G U R E 2 2 : Mithraic bas-relief, originally from Capri and conserved in the Naples Museum. From Amedeo Maiuri, *Capri. Histoire et monuments* (Roma: Instituto poligrafico e zecca dello Stato, 1981), 88.

battle against Christianity. On December 25, this religion celebrated the birth of the sun and represented, in the sacrifice of the bull, the victory of life over the forces of evil. It was a profoundly earthly religion, which did not believe in a beyond and which conceived of the end of the world in the fashion of the Stoics, as a great cosmic conflagration. It was a religion that, in opposition to Christianity, insisted on an affirmation of life.

Nietzsche evokes it precisely during the summer of 1878, during one of the most painful periods of his life, when he seeks to "conquer the evil, bitter elements" and to "fight against illness, vexation, boredom." He will remember this once more when he opens his *Zarathustra* with a dialogue between the protagonist and the sun: "You great star, what would your happiness be had you not those for whom you shine? / For ten years you have climbed to my cave: you would have tired of your light and of the journey had it not been for me and my eagle and my snake."[14]

A second element that is linked to the grotto of Matromania and that Nietzsche had drawn from the work of Gregorovius concerns the interpretation of the Greek verses inscribed on a stele that was found in 1750 in the area surrounding the grotto. Epigraphists today think that it is simply a tombstone, but Gregorovius saw in it the testimony of a human sacrifice made by the emperor Tiberius.

> What terrible crime do the words, so mysterious, inscribed on this child's tomb speak of? There is a secret history of Capri hidden therein. The fate of the poor Hypatos is forgotten, and yet I know it. In a demonic hour, Tiberius sacrificed his favorite child to the sun, here in this cavern, here in this cell. In the same way as Hadrian later sacrificed the beautiful Antinous to the Nile. For at that time human sacrifices, even if they were not made often, were still customary, and most of them were offered to Mithras.[15]

Nietzsche follows Gregorovius's hypothesis and, nine years after the trip to Capri, when discussing religious cruelty in *Beyond Good and Evil*, he refers to the sacrifice of the young Hypatos: "Once one sacrificed human beings to one's god, perhaps precisely those whom one loved most: the sacrifices of the first-born in all prehistoric religions belong here, as well as the sacrifice of the Emperor Tiberius in the Mithras grotto of the isle of Capri, that most gruesome of all Roman anachronisms."[16]

CHAPTER FOUR

Sorrentiner Papiere

As mentioned above, Reinhart von Seydlitz, attracted by the school of educators and by the descriptions of the pleasures of the South, had finally arrived in Sorrento with his wife Irene. Nietzsche had, from the start, established a very friendly and cheerful relationship with the couple. His friend *Rinaldo*, as Nietzsche had nicknamed him, reminisces with nostalgia about the days that they spent together from the end of March to the beginning of May 1877:

> From these dismal days my memory always likes to roam back to those times of Sorrento in the year 1877—"Those were delightful days for me." [. . .] Whenever he entered our room in Sorrento, my wife hurried to prepare the Turkish coffee, which he liked and which so agreed with him. Then he sat in the garden on the terrace or at the piano, and thanked us in his way, giving his best in words or tones. If no outings to Termini, Camaldoli, or Deserto were planned, then a festive "German afternoon" was spent in the orange grove by the ravine, with coffee and pastry, and cheerful chatter. On these afternoons, in a good mood, he used to wear a bright-colored pointed silk Sorrentino cap, remarking that this was the best headgear and most suited to the place. Then he walked with his head leaned back, like a Sorrento prophet, with half-closed eyes, through the avenues of blossoming orange trees. His pace was broad, long, but soft.
>
> And his deep, sonorous, wonderfully melodious voice never uttered an insignificant word. His manner of speaking was undramatic and matter of fact; in the simplest tone of voice he could pronounce sentences which were so seminal and significant that they seemed spoken *sub specie aeterni*.[1]

FIGURE 23 : Reinhardt von Seydlitz circa 1875. GSA 101/437.

Rinaldo also clarifies for us the origin of the philosopher's new book and his new form of writing: "In Sorrento we read to each other aphorisms which we wrote competitively: some of his are in *Things Human, All Too Human*.—'One should be able to have five thoughts per day,' he once said; in this context he used to count the nights as part of the 'days'; and he kept next to his bed a slate tablet on which, in the dark, he jotted down the thoughts that came to him on sleepless nights."[2]

And what of the fifth *Untimely Meditation*? To his editor's letter of February 25, in which he asked Nietzsche for the intended title and release date of the book, the philosopher responds with a postcard, a short quip and a play on words: "Upon *meditation*, don't you think that the *Untimely Meditations* have lost their timeliness?" The poor editor, who was already planning a publicity launch of the five *Untimely Meditations* in one volume, must have thought that his author had lost his mind. However, at the beginning of the journey South, in Bex, Nietzsche was indeed working on the fifth *Untimely*; he spoke of it to the enthusiastic Isabelle on the train and he had dictated parts of it to Brenner. He even announced to his sister that it was finished, and his friends were already talking about it. And the subject of this fifth *Untimely*, the free spirit, could well have served as a transition toward a new phase in his philosophy. But Nietzsche no longer had either the strength or the desire to write it, for it retained the Wagnerian schema of the fight against timeliness for a reform of German culture, and Nietzsche's thought now definitively exited the magic circle of this strange untimeliness, deeply connected to the present. Several years later, he will be fully conscious of this: "If I once wrote the word 'untimely' on my books, how much youth, inexperience, narrowness was inscribed in that word! Today I understand that with this kind of accusation, exaltation, and discontent, I belonged precisely to the most modern of the moderns."[3] In Sorrento, the practice of free thought carried him away and inspired a host of thoughts on the most various subjects, often in the form of aphorisms, which Nietzsche initiated in his notebooks, during his morning walks and which he recopied later in journals or on loose sheets of paper. As we have mentioned, in Weimar there is a file consisting of papers conserved under the name *Sorrentiner Papiere*, the Sorrento papers. It is indeed true that the majority of these pages was written in Sorrento. But it is, in fact, only a final transcription produced by Nietzsche himself and more often by Brenner. As we will see, much more interesting are the Sorrentino notebooks in which thoughts are jotted down in their nascent state, when the philosopher grasped them between the sea and the mountains, between the aroma of the orange trees and that of the sea salt along the narrow paths among the olive trees. And sometimes these thoughts, born in the movement of his walks, retained the colors of the landscape that saw them arise, where, perhaps, they wandered through the air like so many multicolored butterflies.[4]

A new style, a new book, a new phase of his thought . . . For many of Nietzsche's friends, it was not easy to follow the philosopher in this rapid intellectual evolution. Malwida was the first to detect this profound change and to be horrified by it:

One day, Nietzsche arrived with a great bundle of pages written by hand and asked me if I wanted to read them at some point. He told me that they were thoughts that had come to him during his solitary walks; in particular, he indicated a tree to me from which, when he stood under it, a thought would always fall on him. I read the pages with great interest, and there were magnificent thoughts among them, particularly those concerning Greek studies. However, there were others that disconcerted me, that did not at all correspond to Nietzsche as he had been up until that point, and that proved to me that this positivist tendency, whose silent beginnings I had observed throughout the course of the winter, was starting to take root and to give a new shape to his ideas.[5]

Thinking that it was only a temporary phase of his intellectual development, Malwida began by advising him not to publish these drafts right away. Then, when he did publish them, she remained faithful to him, hoping that Nietzsche would eventually change his mind:

We were now faced with the beginnings of the transformation in Nietzsche's thinking. His closest friends first met it with alienation, then almost all of them distanced themselves from him bit by bit, with more or less regret. Yet many, and among them the most significant, did so with indignation and nearly with contempt. I remained faithful to him, because I was firmly convinced that the change that had taken place in him was merely a phase in his development, from which his true spiritual self would emerge evolved and invigorated. [. . .] I hoped that Nietzsche's noble spirit, such as it had shown itself in his beginnings, would be able to overcome these hard conclusions that wandered in all directions, to ugly and untrue extremes, and that only then would he bring his philosophical worldview to maturity in the clear form of a new, sublime ideal.[6]

But the third phase, which Malwida imagined to be a return to the philosophy of *The Birth of Tragedy*, never came, for the good reason that it was precisely the metaphysics of the artist and the critique of culture contained in his writings from the Basel period that constituted the transitory phase in the evolution of Nietzsche's thought. With *Things Human, All Too Human*, Nietzsche had finally recovered his true spiritual nature, his skeptical and immanentist philosophy of the pre-Wagnerian period, which, in the future, far from renouncing, he will only enrich and develop. Even if his dear idealist friend was not entirely aware of it, Nietzsche, for his part, was entirely aware of the break that the Sorrento period represented and of the fact that with *Things Human, All Too Human* he had gotten rid of all that did not belong to him, as he says in *Ecce Homo*: "*Things Human, All Too Human*, this monument of rigorous self-discipline with which I put a sudden end to all my infections with 'higher swindle,' 'idealism,' 'beautiful things,' and other effeminacies, was written in the main in Sorrento; it was finished and received its final form during a winter in Basel, under conditions incomparably less favorable than those in Sorrento."[7] Nietzsche was also aware of the continuity which, in his development, connects his reflections on moral prejudices to the genealogical method of his maturity:

> My ideas on the *origin* of our moral prejudices—for this is the subject of this polemic—received their first, brief, and provisional expression in the collection of aphorisms that bears the title *Things Human, All Too Human: A Book for Free Spirits*. This book was begun in Sorrento during a winter when it was given to me to pause as a wanderer pauses and look back across the broad and dangerous country my spirit had traversed up to that time. This was in the winter of 1876–1877; the ideas themselves are older.[8]

RÉE-ALISM AND THE CHEMICAL COMBINATIONS OF ATOMS

The preliminary drafts of *Things Human, All Too Human* mark, above all, an antimetaphysical turn. In *The Birth of Tragedy* (1872), Nietzsche had constructed a metaphysics of art and the artist affirming that existence is worth living only from an aesthetic perspective. Among the Sorrento papers, there is a very explicit passage on this subject, which we quoted in the introduction: "I want to declare expressly to the readers of my earlier works that I have abandoned the metaphysical-aesthetic views that essentially dominated them: they are pleasant, but untenable."[9] In 1876, Nietzsche renounces the Wagnerian phase, recovers a certain amount of knowledge from his philosophical and philological training, and embraces modern thought, history, and science. In this turn, generally described as positivist, his friendship with Paul Rée plays a central role. The first aphorism of *Things Human, All Too Human*, which practically constitutes the programmatic manifesto of this evolution, contains an autobiographical dimension in the form of a wink to the "school of educators." It is titled "Chemistry of concepts and sensations" and it incites the introduction into philosophy of a rigorous method of analysis taken from a science that embodied, at that time, the cutting edge of scientific knowledge. But it was precisely a feature characteristic of Rée's personality to insist on the chemical combinations of atoms in order to explain the facts of life and the universe. To such an extent that in the little community of the Villa Rubinacci, it had almost become a proverb or a joke:

> [In Sorrento], we had continual discussions with Dr. Rée, a resolute positivist, about philosophical problems, so that the word "chemical combination" ended up becoming a joke among us.[10]
>
> In fact, I just received your little Italian postcard, together with Rée's book, which he finished here. He wrote in it: "To the combination of all good things, the combination of atoms." I always teased him precisely about his dreadfully realist opinions, and when I was speaking with him, instead of saying "human being," I used to say "*the chemical combination*." Now he asserts that no one in the world is good except me and this is what the inscription refers to.[11]

A number of aphorisms in *Things Human, All Too Human* spin a real dialogue with Rée's positivist philosophy, a dialogue with points of contact and a certain amount of inexplicit divergences that will manifest more strongly later on. When *Things Human, All Too Human* was published in 1878, most of his friends hardly appreciated Nietzsche's positivist shift and attributed it to the bad influence of *The Origin of the Moral Sensations*, the book that Rée wrote in Sorrento. As for Rée himself, he was overjoyed when he read Nietzsche's book. In it, he saw a development on the largest scale of many shared concerns, with an unequaled nobility of perspective, a genius composed of multiple talents that came together in a singular vision.

> Oh, dearest friend, what a marvelous surprise! I am beside myself and plunged straight into it like a hungry beast of prey. These matters, which are the most interesting of all to me, associated with a thousand personal memories and connections in nearly every sentence, truly make it the book of books for me. I feel like a man living something that he had previously dreamed of—he had already experienced, heard, read everything somewhere—just as I had heard so many things from you in person or read them in the Sorrento manuscript—but it was half-forgotten again, like the memory of a dream, and now it stands before me as an incarnate reality. And what a reality! I see my own self, projected outside of me on an enlarged scale. Allow me the impertinence to tell you what kind of a man you are: precisely not a man but a conglomerate of men—while each of your so variously gifted friends agonizes to support his talent—the singular talent that he possesses—and to give it prestige, thus exhausting all of his strength, you have all of these different talents, sometimes greater, sometimes

equally great to that of every other individual. In particular, I have luxuriated in *Of Christian holiness and asceticism.*[12] If the Germans do not become friends with the psychologists, I shall emigrate to France. [. . .] I have never been so pleasantly surprised in all my life. A thousand salutations and thanks![13]

The reception at Bayreuth was very different: "Richard reads some of Nietzsche's latest book and is astonished by its pretentious ordinariness. 'I can understand why Rée's company is more congenial to him than mine.' And when I remark that to judge by this book Nietzsche's earlier ones were just reflections [*Reflexe*] of something else, they did not come from within, he says, 'And now they are Rée-flections [*Réeklekse*]!'"[14] Cosima, in a letter to Marie von Schleinitz, did not fail to emphasize the bad Jewish influence: "Many things went to the making of this miserable book! Last of all Jewry, in the person of one Dr. Rée—a very sleek, very cold person, to all appearance entirely influenced and dominated by Nietzsche, but in reality making a dupe of him—an illustration on a small scale of the relation between Judea and Germania."[15]

Erwin Rohde, his friend and fellow student, the other "Wagnerian professor" who was destined to become one of the most important Hellenists of his time, wrote to Nietzsche: "My surprise at this most recent *Nietzschianum* was, as you can imagine, the greatest possible: as it inevitably must be when one is thrown from the *calidarium* straight into an ice-cold *frigidarium*! I will tell you now in all candor, my friend, that this surprise did not come without painful feelings. Is it possible to remove one's own soul *in this way* and to assume that of another? Instead of Nietzsche, to suddenly become Rée? I still stand astonished at this miracle, and can neither be happy about it nor have a specific opinion about it, because I have not yet properly *understood* it."[16] Nietzsche responded with a beautiful letter in which he expresses his friendship to Rohde and, simultaneously, explains the significance and the limits of his new friendship with Rée and their mutual intellectual exchange:

> All of this is well and good, my dear friend: we are *not* yet standing together on a clay pedestal that can be overturned by a book.
>
> This time, I am quietly waiting for the waves in which my poor friends are floundering to die down: if I pushed them into these waves—*life* is not in danger, I know that from experience; and if, here and there, *friendship* might be in *danger*—then we will serve the truth and say: "as yet, we have loved only a cloud of one another."
>
> There would be many things to *say*, and even more ineffable things to *think*: in jest, allow me to simply venture a comparison. I am like a man who has

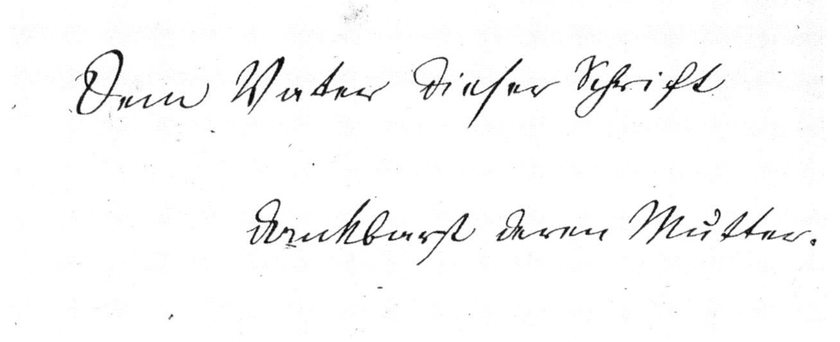

FIGURE 24: Rée's inscription to Nietzsche: "Dem Vater dieser Schrift dankbarst dessen Mutter." Herzogin Anna Amalia Bibliothek, shelf mark C 309.

prepared an elaborate feast, with a great many succulent dishes, and whose guests, at the sight of them, immediately run away. If one or another of them finds at least a morsel to be to their liking (as you do, dear friend, in honoring the Greeks[17]), this man will feel satisfied.

Do not muse over the origin of such a book, but continue instead to help yourself here and there to what you like. Perhaps the time will come one day when you, with your beautiful constructivist fantasy, will see the whole as a whole and will be able to partake in the great fortune that *I* have enjoyed until now.

Parenthetically: always look for *me* in my book and not my friend Rée. I am proud to have discovered these magnificent qualities and aspirations, but he did not have the *slightest* influence on the conception of my "*philosophia in nuce*": this was *ready* and, in great part, already entrusted to paper when I made his acquaintance, in the autumn of 1876. We found one another on the same level: the pleasure of our conversations was immeasurable and certainly the gain was very great from both sides (to such an extent that Rée, with affectionate exaggeration, wrote to me in *his* book, *The Origin of the Moral Sensations*, "to the father of this writing, from its grateful mother").

Perhaps, by saying this, I seem even more unfamiliar, even more incomprehensible to you? If only you felt what I feel now, since I have finally posed my ideal of life—the fresh, pure air of *altitudes*, the balmy warmth surrounding me—then you could rejoice very, very much for your friend. And that day too *will come*.

With all my heart,
your F.[18]

The day of the intellectual and human reunion between Nietzsche and Rohde will never come. Their correspondence will become more and more sporadic until their break in 1887, a consequence of Rohde's negative judgment of Hippolyte Taine.[19]

The ideal of life that the philosopher had posed for himself after the publication of his "scandalous" book is more clearly expressed in a letter responding to another disappointed Wagnerian, Mathilde Maier. She had written him a long letter:

> You can hardly imagine the deep agitation that your book has caused me, how many sleepless nights I've had on its account! [. . .] When a spirit like yours, so invested in the ideal, and with, I believe, an exceptionally strong metaphysical need, arrives by other paths [than naïve materialism] at the dictum: the philosophy of the future will be identical to natural science—how am I not to be profoundly shocked! [. . .] We constructed a godless religion with pain and hardship to save the divine when we had lost God—and now you pull away the very foundation that, as airy and nebulous as it may be, was strong enough to support an entire world, the world of all that is dear and sacred to us! Metaphysics is only an illusion; but what is life without this illusion? [. . .] The most horrifying thing for me is the annihilation of the eternal idea, the one source of peace and protection in the face of eternal becoming! And now you have destroyed everything! A world in flux, no more stable images, only a single, eternal movement! It's enough to go insane![20]

Nietzsche responds to her on July 15, speaking of the intellectual and material genesis of his book:

> My dear Fräulein Maier,
>
>   It cannot be changed: I must create distress for all of my friends—precisely as I finally express how I saved myself *from* distress. That metaphysical way of obscuring all that is true and simple, the battle *with* reason *against* reason, which wants to see in each and every thing a miracle and an absurdity—along with that, the corresponding baroque art of excessive tension and glorified exorbitance—I mean Wagner's art—these two things were what made me sick and sicker, and nearly alienated me from my good temperament and talent. If you could only feel the pure air of the *altitudes* that I live in *now*, the sweet sentiment toward the people who still dwell in the mist of the valleys, more than ever devoted as I am to all that is good and active, a hundred steps closer to the Greeks than I ever have been; and how I *myself* now *live* striving for wisdom to

the smallest detail, while before I only worshipped and idolized *the wise*—in short, if you could undergo as I have this transformation and crisis, then you *would have* to desire to live something like it.

It was during the summer in Bayreuth that I became fully conscious of it: after the first performances that I attended, I fled to the mountains and there, in a small village in the forest, the first draft came into being, approximately a third of my book, at that time titled "The Plowshare." Then, following my sister's desire, I returned to Bayreuth and had the inner composure to bear the nearly unbearable—keeping *quiet* in front of everyone! *Now* I cast off all that is not part *of me*: people, be they friends or enemies, habits, comforts, books; I live in solitude, and shall for years to come, until, as a philosopher of *life*, mature and ready, I will be *allowed* (and probably also *obligated*) to communicate with people once again.[21]

THE LOGIC OF DREAMS

Let us return now to the Sorrentino manuscripts in order to read several more of these fragments or aphorisms that retain an echo of the places and travel companions in Sorrento, transposed into a philosophical context. In a long and important aphorism from the first part of *Things Human, All Too Human*, titled "Logic of the dream," Nietzsche inserts and links together two personal experiences: one of them distant, recovered from the drawers of memory, and the other very recent, which formed the origin of this philosophical reflection, that of the bells of Sorrento. The aphorism, number thirteen of *Things Human, All Too Human*, begins with a description of the unusual position that the sleeper's body takes. This position, by virtue of its exceptional nature, excites the entirety of the nervous system, including cerebral functioning. And thus, Nietzsche continues,

there are a hundred occasions for the mind to be involved in puzzlement and to look for *grounds* for this excitation: the dream is the *seeking and representation of the causes* of this excitement of the sensibilities, that is to say the supposed causes. If, for example, you tie two straps about your feet you may well dream that your feet are coiled round by snakes: this is first a hypothesis, then a belief, with an accompanying pictorial representation and the supposition: "these snakes must be the *causa* of those sensations that I, the sleeper, feel"—thus the sleeper's mind judges. The immediate past he had thus inferred becomes through his aroused imagination the present to him. Everyone knows from experience how quickly a dreamer entwines with his dream a sound that

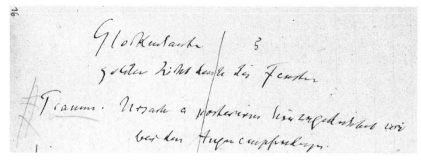

FIGURE 25: Nietzsche, notebook N II 3, page 36. GSA 71/175.

strongly impinges upon him from without, the ringing of bells or the firing of a cannon, for example; that is to say, he accounts for the sound in terms of the dream, so that he *believes* he experiences the cause of the sound first, then the sound itself.[22]

The origin of this aphorism can be found, in fact, in a brief notation in the Sorrento notebooks: "Sounds of a bell—golden light through the window. Dream. Cause written in a posteriori as in visual sensations."[23] This is explained by the life habits of the group of friends, described very well by Albert Brenner's account:

At 6:15 in the morning, everything is completely silent inside and outside the house; only the doors creak in the wind. At 6:30, a dismal and sorrowful sound rings out from the chapel near us. Soon after, a voice cries: "Brenner!" No answer. Deathly silence. The sorrowful bell whines again. Silence. After several minutes: "Brenner!" Brief silence. Then the response: "oh, oh, oh—." Silence again. Then once more, louder: "Brenner!" Awkward silence. "What? Yes! I'm getting up!"[24]

At the hour when the bell of Sorrento resounds, while his friend is awkwardly rising out of sleep, Nietzsche reflects upon the logic of dreams. This recent impression combines with a distant memory, a memory that had resurfaced for Nietzsche during a period of return to his past. In fact, at the age of fourteen, he had entrusted to his journal of his years as a student at the school of Pforta: "It is astonishing how active the imagination is in dreams: since I always wear elastic bands on my socks at night, I dreamed that two snakes had coiled around my legs, I caught one of them by the head, awoke, and found myself with a sock suspender in my hands."[25]

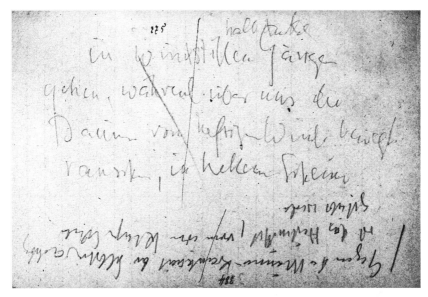

FIGURE 26: Nietzsche, notebook N II 3, page 15. GSA 71/175.

AN EPICUREAN IN SORRENTO

On his walks, the paths of Sorrento themselves provide Nietzsche with material to translate his thoughts into images. And he jots down in his notebook: "Walking along the windless, twilight pathways, while above us the trees rustle, agitated by violent gales in a brighter light."[26]

In a letter to Reinhart von Seydlitz, the philosophical content of this image is unveiled a bit further: "Foreigners are beginning to flock to Sorrento; March is generally considered to be the month that draws the most of them. We discovered in the past few days, by experience, that it can actually be *stormy* here. They say that the beautiful season starts in March, but we will surely not be spared a couple of windy days. There are such wonderful walks on paths where one is sheltered among the orange trees, and comforted by a constant calm. Only in the agitation among the pines *above* does one *see* that on the outside, in the world, a storm is raging (reality and allegory of our local life—*true* in both senses)."[27] Afterward, this same image allows him to rediscover and to better characterize one of the great antitheses of the philosophical tradition, that opposing the Cynics and the Epicureans, which he presents in aphorism 275 of *Things Human, All Too Human*:

> The Epicurean likewise employs his higher culture to make himself independent of dominating opinions; only he lifts himself above them, while the Cynic

remains at the stage of negation. It is as though he [the Epicurean] wanders along still, sheltered, twilight pathways, while above him the tops of the trees whirl about in the wind and betray to him how violently buffeted the world outside is. In the case of the Cynic, on the other hand, it is as though he walks abroad naked in the teeth of the wind and hardens himself to the point of feeling nothing.[28]

Renate Müller-Buck saw in the description of the Cynic who "remains at the stage of negation" a portrait of Albert Brenner—which would make of this aphorism not only an evocation of the landscape of Sorrento, but also a literary monument to the memory of the young man, prematurely deceased. It is easy to guess who the Epicurean was . . .

SACRED MUSIC ON AN AFRICAN BACKGROUND

Surrounded by the inhabitants of a small Southern village, he finds himself struck by various details of daily life, which inspire him to make observations such as the following:

> *Industriousness in South and North.* —Industriousness originates in two quite different ways. Craftsmen in the South are industrious, not from a desire for gain, but because others are always in need. Because someone always comes along who wants a horse shod, a cart repaired, the smith is always industrious. If no one came along, he would lounge about in the marketplace. To feed himself in a fruitful country requires no great effort: a very moderate amount of work will suffice, in any event he has no need for industriousness; ultimately he would beg and be content. —The industriousness of English workers, on the other hand, has behind it the sense for gain: it is aware of itself and of its objectives, and desires with possessions power, with power the greatest possible freedom and individual nobility.[29]

Or, venturing outside of the village, Nietzsche could arrive by chance in the middle of a scene so strange and unreal that it allowed him to understand the hidden absurdity of such mundane and regular experiences as listening to music. "Dear Olga," Malwida writes to her adoptive daughter,

> we just got back from a long ride on donkeys (Rée and Nietzsche were on horseback), for the first time since the divine weather has returned; we went up to the mountains above the Gulf of Salerno, where one can see both gulfs

on the two sides of the country, with the mountains of Calabria still covered in snow, looking sublime beneath the blue sky; the Gulf of Salerno, even more Southern and even bluer than the Gulf of Naples, all dotted with flowers; before us, the little isles of the sirens that lie enchantingly below, and around us, as we sat up there, a band of children who were nearly African, with brown skin, black eyes, white teeth, laughed in our direction, brought us flowers and finally sang—it was terribly funny—a so-called religious song, with the refrain: *Viva, viva il cuor di Maria, Eviva Dio che tanto l'amà*. Isn't that deliciously pagan and sensual? It was a divine morning and we all enjoyed it very much.[30]

The refrain of this sacred song reappears one year later, in a notebook of Nietzsche's:

Tower near Sorrento on the mountain of the domestic ape

> *evviva evviva il cuor di Maria*
> *evviva il Dio que tanto l'ama.*

And in another notebook of the same period, the philosopher writes:

A refrain (Sorrento) is felt by us against a *false background* [*falschen Folie*]: *so it is* with *all* music of the past.[31]

That day, on the Sorrentino peninsula, while riding on horseback between the two gulfs, Nietzsche glimpsed the inconsistency between a form of music and the scenery that accompanies it. He sensed the profound dissonance between the pagan scene of these smiling children and the Christian hymn they sang. In the note written one year later, the philosopher generalized this personal experience and saw therein the inevitable incomprehension that comes with all music when it is not heard against the background of the cultural and social landscape of the era that produced it. Let us remark in passing that in order to bring across his idea, he used the term *Folie* (background, setting, scenery), which the German language borrowed from a dance of Iberian origin, from the sixteenth century, the *folia*. Similar to the chaconne and the sarabande, this dance, which circulated throughout Europe, was used in the eighteenth century to give musical form to interludes or for the initial and final scenes of an opera. For the eighteenth century, therefore, the term *folia* indicates not only the music but the scenes themselves, the stage sets of these interludes. Afterward, this word remains in the German language, retaining only the latter meaning. Nietzsche knowingly uses a rare term of musical and theatrical origin, a term just as anachronistic as the song of these children. This concept resurfaces in an extremely important aphorism of *Assorted Opinions and Maxims* (whose draft can be found among the Sorrento papers). Nietzsche uses it as a weapon of argument against the Schopenhauerian and Wagnerian doctrine that made music a universal language of emotion and the singular means of communication that would bind men together beyond space and time.

> Music is thus *not* a universal language for all ages [*überzeitliche*], as has so often been claimed for it, but accords precisely with a measure of time, warmth, and sensibility that a quite distinct individual culture, limited as to area and duration, bears within it as an inner law: the music of Palestrina would be wholly inaccessible to a Greek, and conversely—what would Palestrina hear in the music of Rossini?[32]

THE SUN OF KNOWLEDGE AND THE GROUND OF THINGS

During his Sorrentino retreat, the philosopher gathers other images and metaphors, which help him to better define the figure of the free-spirited philosopher, his love of knowledge, and his social position. Let us read one of these images, posed, as usual, in three short phrases jotted down in the Sorrento notebooks.

> Sunlight glistens on the ground and shows what the waves flow over: craggy rocks.
>
> What matters is how much breath you have to plunge into this element: if you have a lot of it, then you'll be able to see the ground.
>
> The glistening sunshine of knowledge cascades through the flux of things, down to their ground.[33]

And this is how this image passes into the text of *Things Human, All Too Human*, in the penultimate aphorism of the chapter dedicated to the free spirit:

> The free spirited, men who live for the sake of knowledge alone, will find they soon attain the external goal of their life, their definitive position in relation to society and the state, and will easily be content with, for example, a minor office or an income that just enables them to live; for they will organize their life in such a way that a great transformation of external circumstances, even

an overturning of the political order, does not overturn their life with it. Upon all these things they expend as little energy as possible, so that they may dive down into the element of knowledge with all their accumulated strength and as it were with a deep breath. Thus they may hope to dive deep and perhaps get a view of the ground at the bottom.[34]

THE BLESSED ISLES

From the terrace of the Villa Rubinacci, Nietzsche sees, every day, far off in the distance, in the sea between Mount Vesuvius and Capri, the rugged silhouette of the Isle of Ischia.[35] As he reflects upon the school of educators, on the civilization of free spirits and the project of creating a place for the training of higher men, he has before him this volcanic, fertile island, rife with history. This image, which is not mentioned in the Sorrento manuscripts, remains, however, imprinted in his mind and reemerges over the course of the following years, in an extremely important passage in his body of work. Nietzsche will say so himself, seven years later. In the summer of 1883, at Malwida's suggestion, Nietzsche had planned to go and live on the Isle of Ischia with his sister, but on July 28, a violent earthquake had destroyed a considerable portion of the island, in particular the localities of Casamicciola and Lacco Ameno. In his description of this event to Heinrich Köselitz, Nietzsche reveals the particular meaning that this island has always had for him:

> The fate of Ischia shocks me more and more; and aside from what concerns everyone else, there is something about it that touches me personally, in a haunting way that is entirely my own. This island was so present in my thought: once you have read *Zarathustra II* to the end, it will be clear to you *where* I sought my "blessed isles." "Cupid dancing with the young girls" is immediately comprehensible only in Ischia (the women of Ischia say "Cupedo"). I have hardly finished my poem when the island collapses.[36]

In *Thus Spoke Zarathustra*, the blessed isles are those where Zarathustra's disciples live. And this is not a mere detail, but a constitutive element of the Zarathustrian pedagogical process. Indeed, in the book's prologue, Zarathustra attempts to preach to the crowd in the marketplace using a simplified language, adapted for the purpose of mass communication.[37] But he is misunderstood and made into an object of ridicule; the only result of this is that he finds himself with a corpse on his shoulders, that is, an ardent disciple unable to move on his own—a heap of dead weight. Zarathustra understands, then, that he must not speak to the people, but to his companions, and that he needs living companions, who follow him because they desire to follow themselves, and not dead companions that he must drag along at his will. He understands that his task is not to become the shepherd of a herd but to persuade a great many individuals to diverge from the herd: "Companions, the creator seeks, not corpses, not herds and believers. Fellow creators, the creator seeks—those who write new values on new tablets."[38] Zarathustra's speeches that follow the prologue thus serve to educate his disciples. Zarathustra summarizes, therein, the philosophy of the free spirit.[39] Zarathustra preaches against absolute truths and for individual virtues, he historicizes morality and rehabilitates the values of the body, seeks to reinforce the instinctual structure of the individual to give him the capacity to create. Zarathustra's speeches are thus addressed to men who consider themselves to be above the commonplace values, established lies, and petty virtues upon which mediocrity is founded and who, by remaining in society, run the risk of losing their highest hopes. Nietzsche offers these men an educational path that develops individual drives and talents in a balanced fashion, by following new and original configurations. As he will later write: "To become master of the chaos that one is; to force one's chaos to become form; to become necessity in form: to become logical, simple, unequivocal, mathematical; to become *law*—: that is the great ambition."[40] The freedom of the spirit and the will to power do not lead, according to Nietzsche, to an explosion of existing instincts, to a laisser-aller, or to a return to an imagined originary innocence: "not to confuse libertinage,[41] the principle of 'laisser-aller'[42] with the *will to power* (—which is the *opposite* principle)"[43]; and even less, naturally, to their suppression: "Sovereignty over the passions, *not* their weakening or eradication! The greater the power of mastery of our will, the greater the freedom we may give to the passions. The great man is great by the margin of freedom that he gives to his cravings: but he is strong enough to make of these monsters his domestic animals."[44]

In the last speech of the first part, Zarathustra summarizes the nature of this new "gift-giving virtue" that his disciples must acquire: "Power is she, this new virtue; a dominant thought is she, and around her a wise soul: a golden sun, and around it the serpent of knowledge."[45] Above all, Zarathustra does not give his disciples a morality to follow. He asks them only to create worldviews and ways of life that do not strive toward the supernatural: "Remain faithful to the earth, my brothers, with the power of your virtue. Let your gift-giving love and your knowledge serve the meaning of the earth. Thus I beg and beseech you. [. . .] Lead back to earth the virtue that flew away, as I do—back to the body, back to life, that it may give earth a meaning, a human meaning."[46] And he concludes by addressing to his disciples a harsh and urgent call to independence and skepticism:

> Now I go alone, my disciples. You too go now, alone. Thus I want it. [. . .]
> You say you believe in Zarathustra? But what matters Zarathustra? You are my
> believers—but what matter all believers? You had not yet sought yourselves:
> and you found me. Thus do all believers; therefore all faith amounts to so little.
>
> Now I bid you lose me and find yourselves; and only when you have all
> denied me will I return to you.[47]

Heinrich Köselitz, in response to the first part of *Zarathustra*, which Nietzsche had sent him, confessed that he detected in the book an unjustified contempt for humanity, while on the contrary, in his opinion, the wise man must always arrive at the conclusion "that he and the world are complementary."[48] Nietzsche responds to him very frankly: "My conviction is that there are higher and lower human beings, and many grades and distances between them; and it is essential that the higher human being not only *stand* on a higher level but that he feel the *affect of distance* and, occasionally, that he reveal it—essential at least so that his higher being is *active*, and therefore *moves* still higher. If I entirely understand the first *Zarathustra*, it wishes to appeal to those who, living amid the throng and the rabble, *either* completely become the *sacrifices* of this distance-affect (from nausea, in some cases!) *or* must dispose of this affect: it tells them to seek refuge either on a solitary blessed isle—or in Venice."[49]

Sure enough, at the beginning of the second part of *Zarathustra*, we discover that his disciples have indeed left for the blessed isles. Isolation and solitude constitute the first and essential step toward the liberation of the spirit because they allow us to step back from dominant ideas so as to analyze and modify them. Hence the importance of the image of the blessed isles, which is constantly present in the four parts of *Zarathustra*. At the beginning of the second part, we learn that Zarathustra's doctrine has been transformed by his enemies. So Zarathustra sets out on a journey to join his disciples and continue his teaching. "Like a cry and a shout of joy I want to sweep over wide seas, till I find the blessed isles where my friends are dwelling. And my enemies among them! How I now love all to whom I may speak! My enemies too are part of my bliss."[50] We thus learn in passing that not only Zarathustra's disciples, but his enemies, too, live on the blessed isles—a confirmation that this is an unorthodox utopia. The whole teaching of the second part of *Zarathustra* takes place "Upon the Blessed Isles," as the title of the second parable indicates. In the parable "The Dancing Song," Zarathustra strikes up "a satirical song on the spirit of gravity, my supreme and most powerful devil, of whom they say that he is 'the master of the world'" while Cupid and the young girls dance together.[51] And, as Nietzsche wrote in the letter to Köselitz quoted above, "'Cupid dancing with the young girls' is immediately comprehensible only in Ischia."

The third part opens on Zarathustra's journey from the blessed isles to his dwelling. Zarathustra goes home because he must confront his last overcoming, he must evoke the thought of the eternal return and accept it. The happiness and the love for his children that keep him on the island is a kind of bliss that comes too early and postpones the time when his maturation is meant to come. Already on the boat that brings him back home, "The Vision and the Riddle" of the eternal return appear to him after four days of travel, and he becomes aware of the danger that he risked on the blessed isles: the danger of softening and of neglecting his mission. One outline in particular is revealing:

> Zarathustra 3 beginning. Recapitulation. You want to teach the overman—but you have fallen in love with your friends and yourself and you have made a refreshment of life. The blessed isles make you effeminate—now you grow *dim* and ardent, you scold your enemies. A sign of weakness: you evade a thought.
>
> But you must persuade the world and persuade the human being to shatter himself.
>
> (The reformer slackens in his own community: his enemies are not strong enough. And so a greater enemy must emerge for him, a thought. Thought as an argument *against* life and survival).[52]

The published text, titled "On Involuntary Bliss," explains that the happy medium found on the blessed isles must be broken in order to allow for the development of Zarathustra's personality and that of his disciples to continue. Indeed, despite the fact that the disciples enjoy life in the community of free spirits, they still require solitude in order to mature: "My children are still verdant in their first spring, standing close together and shaken by the same winds—the trees of my garden and my best soil. And verily, where such trees stand together there *are* blessed isles. But one day I want to dig them up and place each by itself, so it may learn solitude and defiance and caution." Zarathustra too must return to his solitude to accomplish his task and become the master of the eternal return: "Thus I am in the middle of my work, going to my children and returning from them: for his children's sake, Zarathustra must perfect himself. [. . .] Therefore I now evade my happiness and offer myself to all unhappiness, for *my own* final testing and knowledge. [. . .] Alas, thought of the abyss that is *my* thought, when shall I find the strength to hear you digging, without trembling anymore? My heart pounds to my very throat whenever I hear you digging. Even your silence wants to choke me, you who are silent from the abyss."[53]

The blessed isles emerge once again in the fourth part of *Thus Spoke Zarathustra*. In the second parable, the soothsayer, who represents the sorrow of the man who has lost all hope of changing the world, says to Zarathustra, sighing, that "all is the same, nothing is worthwhile, no seeking avails, nor are there any blessed isles anymore."[54] In the drafts of this episode, written shortly after the earthquake of 1883 in Ischia, Nietzsche had even staged the destruction of the blessed isles: "The sinking of the blessed isles *awakes* him."[55] Zarathustra, in any case, has not lost hope in the future of humanity, and the blessed isles incarnate precisely his hopefulness: "'No! No! Three times no!' he shouted with a strong voice and stroked his beard. '*That* I know better: there still are blessed isles. Be quiet about *that*, you sighing bag of sadness!'"[56] Further on, when all of the higher men are gathered in Zarathustra's cave, the blessed isles are evoked once again in a very significant context. The higher men represent the great figures of contemporary European decadence and are characterized by their disgust for existence and contempt for humanity.[57] Zarathustra sees them coming toward him:

> And that we who were despairing have now come to your cave and no longer despair—that is but a sign and symbol that those better than we are on their way to you; for this is what is on its way to you: the last remnant of God among men—that is, all the men of great longing, of great nausea, of great disgust, all who do not want to live unless they learn to *hope* again, unless they learn from you, O Zarathustra, the *great* hope.[58]

But Zarathustra asserts very clearly that it is not for them that he was waiting in the mountains: "You may indeed all be higher men [. . .], but for me you are not high and strong enough." It is for other men that Zarathustra waited in his mountains: "those who are higher, stronger, more triumphant, and more cheerful, such as are built perpendicular in body and soul: *laughing lions* must come! [. . .] Speak to me of my gardens, of my blessed isles, of my new, beautiful species—why do you not speak to me of that? This present I beseech from your love, that you speak to me of my children. For this I am rich, for this I grew poor; what did I not give, what would I not give to have one thing: these children, this living plantation, these life-trees of my will and my highest hope!"[59] At the end of the fourth part, even if Zarathustra's sons do not come, a sign that they are approaching will nonetheless arrive from the blessed isles: a laughing lion surrounded by a flight of doves, a symbol of the greatest power, which does not manifest as violence but in the form of a laugh accompanied by peace and love:

> "*The sign is at hand*," said Zarathustra, and a change came over his heart. And indeed, as it became light before him, a mighty yellow animal lay at his feet and pressed its head against his knees and out of love did not want to let go of him, and acted like a dog that finds its old master again. But the doves were no less eager in their love than the lion; and whenever a dove slipped over the lion's nose, the lion shook its head and was amazed and laughed.[60]

From this brief trajectory, the role that the blessed isles play in *Thus Spoke Zarathustra* appears clearly. But why did Nietzsche choose this expression and why did he choose Ischia as his model? The isle is the location of utopia par excellence, of experimentation with new possibilities of existence. The image of the blessed isles in particular comes from a tradition of thirty centuries and spread throughout all of the peoples of the Mediterranean, especially among the Greeks and the Romans, but probably also among the Phoenicians and the Carthaginians. Possessing a similar function to Homer's Elysian Fields, the blessed isles (in Greek, μακάρων νῆσοι) are located at the edges of the world and enjoy a prosperous and uniform climate and luxurious vegetation that yields three harvests a year with no need to till the earth. Hesiod, who borrows the Homeric place and uses the name of the isles of the blessed for the first time, relates that Zeus reserved them for the brave representatives of the race of heroes, those who escaped death on the battlefield.[61]

As a result of his training and his professorship of classical philology, Nietzsche naturally knew these texts and many others on the blessed isles and consciously inserts himself into this tradition, which reveals, among other things, the Greek heritage of *Thus Spoke Zarathustra*.[62] Already before *Thus Spoke Zarathustra*, Nietzsche had used the image of the isle as a place in which to gather a small community of friends and to train the educators of a new civilization. In the beginning, the project is closely tied to the atmosphere of the villa at Tribschen, where the Wagners lived in the early 1870s and where Nietzsche came often from Basel to visit them and speak of the future. A letter to Erwin Rohde of 1870 allows us to catch a glimpse of the many hopes that stirred up the young Basel professor's mind:

> Let us drag ourselves through this university existence for two more years, let us take it as an *instructive sorrow* that we must bear seriously and with aston-

ishment. It must be an *educational* time during which we learn to *teach*, and I consider it my task to train myself for teaching. Except that I have set the goal a bit higher for myself. [. . .] Thus one day we will cast off this yoke—*for me* this is entirely certain. Then we shall found a new *Greek* Academy [. . .]. You probably already know from your visit to Tribschen about *Wagner's* plan for Bayreuth. [. . .] Even if we find only few companions who share our views, I still believe that we will be able—with some losses, of course—to pull ourselves out of this current and reach a small isle, where we will no longer need to stuff wax in our ears. Then we will teach one another, our books will only be the fishhook to attract someone to our monastic artistic community. We will live, work, be happy through one another—perhaps that will be the only way for us to work for the *whole*.[63]

Unfortunately, the Tribschen dream had collapsed at Bayreuth, when Nietzsche had realized that the isle of knowledge and of the education of higher men had been transformed into a seaport of society life, where the artist sought to dominate the masses by exploiting nationalism and religion:

I loved the man, his way of living as if on an isle and of *closing himself off* from the world without hate: this is the way I understood it! How remote it has become, now that, swimming in the current of nationalist greed and nationalist venom, he desires to accommodate the need for religion of these contemporary *peoples*, made stupid by politics and cupidity! I once thought that he had nothing to do with the men of today—I was indeed a fool.[64]

When, in *Ecce Homo*, Nietzsche relates the birth of *Things Human, All Too Human*, and the disillusionment of Bayreuth, he refers to the Tribschen era:

The beginnings of this book belong right in the midst of the first *Bayreuther Festspiele*; a profound alienation from everything that surrounded me there is one of its preconditions. Whoever has any notion of the visions I had encountered even before that may guess how I felt when one day I woke up in Bayreuth. As if I were dreaming! Wherever was I? There was nothing I recognized; I scarcely recognized Wagner. In vain did I leaf through my memories. Tribschen—a distant isle of the blessed: not a trace of any similarity.[65]

When Wagner moves, both physically and metaphorically, from Tribschen to Bayreuth, the Nietzschean dream of the blessed isles travels to the South. But why does the philosopher choose Ischia in particular as a model? We do not have any formal explanations on Nietzsche's part, but we can underline certain historical and geographical elements and attempt to explain the role of this isle in the Nietzschean imaginary by bringing it face to face with another Zarathustrian isle.

Historically, Ischia is the first Greek settlement in Italy, founded under the name of Pithekoussai by Greek colonists from the isle of Euboea at the beginning of the eighth century BCE. In the era of Hesiod, it represented the westernmost Greek settlement and thus it was truly located at the edges of the known world. Some scholars think that Ischia is the isle where Odysseus met Nausicaa. Nietzsche would have been delighted to know that a vase called Nestor's Cup, which bears one of the most ancient Greek inscriptions, has recently been discovered in Ischia. Even from a geographical perspective, the isle corresponds to the antique literary descriptions, because its very fertile ground produces a plentiful Mediterranean vegetation: grapevines, olive trees, citrus fruits, and grains. Its temperate climate has a moderate thermal range between fifty and seventy-three degrees and minimal humidity. Nietzsche is struck, moreover, by the volcanic nature of the isle of Ischia. In the process of constructing the image of a place in which ideas marking a detachment from tradition develop, the power that rises from volcanic earth is an important element. In a brief note written at the end of the Sorrentino period, we read: "On volcanic soil, everything thrives."[66] For Nietzsche, new ideas guide and accelerate historical development, and the deviance of the free spirit must be encouraged.[67] But at the same time, the isle of Ischia is distinct from another isle discussed in Zarathustra's parable titled "On Great Events": the isle of the fire hound, with its continually smoking volcano, just as the free spirit is distinct from the revolutionary.

> There is an island in the sea—not far from Zarathustra's blessed isles—on which a fire-spewing mountain smokes continually; and the people say of it, and especially the old women among the people say, that it has been placed like a huge rock before the gate to the underworld, and that the narrow path that leads to this gate to the underworld goes through the fire-spewing mountain.[68]

On the isle of the volcano, there lives a fire hound, which represents "all of the overthrow- and scum-demons."[69] Zarathustra speaks to him and derides him. In the drafts, we read: "Conversation with the *fire hound*. Ridicule of his pathos. Against revolution." "Ridicule of revolutions and of Vesuvius. Something of the surface."[70] For Zarathustra, the idea that it is possible to change the life of men and to make it move forward by means of a violent act is an illusion.

FIGURE 27 A: The Isle of Ischia as seen from the terrace of the Villa Rubinacci. Picture kindly provided by the directors of the Hotel Eden.

Revolutionary change does not affect the depths and changes merely the surface appearance of things. Often, after a revolution, after being overturned in the mud, the statues of the past dominant power present themselves as victims and resurface from the mud even younger than before. The action of the free spirit, on the contrary, aims to produce a transformation that is not violent but more profound, which acts within the sphere of values:

> Not around the inventors of new noise, but around the inventors of new values does the world revolve; it revolves *inaudibly*.
>
> Admit it! Whenever your noise and smoke were gone, very little had happened. What does it matter if a city became a mummy and a statue lies in the mud? [. . .]
>
> The statue lay in the mud of your contempt; but precisely this is its law, that out of contempt, it grows new life and living beauty.[71]

At the end of the second part, when Zarathustra doubts himself and his mission and says that he does not have the lion's voice necessary to command men, a response comes to him in a whisper: "It is the stillest words that bring on the storm. Thoughts that come on doves' feet guide the world."[72]

The fire hound returns, ashamed, to his cave when Zarathustra tells him that there exists another fire hound, who digs out gold and laughter from the heart of the earth and whose face emanates not pillars of smoke, of ash, and of mud but "laughter [. . .] like colorful clouds."[73]

Even without what the drafts tell us, we clearly recognize Mount Vesuvius in the description of the fire hound's island. Of course, Vesuvius is not located

L'Eruzione del Vesuvio, 26 Aprile 1872 ore 3, P. M.   N° 6102

FIGURE 27 B : The eruption of Vesuvius in 1872. Photo George Sommer.

on an island, but if one looks at it from Sorrento, it seems to form something like an isle in the Gulf of Naples, on the right, a twin to the isle of Ischia, which is found on the left. From his terrace at the Villa Rubinacci, Nietzsche could gaze, day after day, at the two "isles": the isle of Ischia, the model of the blessed isles occupied by the free spirits, and the isle of Vesuvius, occupied by the fire hound. Each of them is volcanic: except that on the blessed isles the volcano is an instrument of gradual transformation that serves to set in motion and accelerate a process of development. On the other hand, on the isle of the fire hound, the volcano's eruption destroys the city, mummifies its inhabitants (Pompeii), overturns the statues, and changes everything so that nothing changes.

CHAPTER FIVE

The Bells of Genoa
and Nietzschean Epiphanies

Nietzsche had come to Sorrento to recover—in vain. Nietzsche's rare post-cards and Rée's long letters sent to Naumburg, to Franziska and to Eliza-beth Nietzsche, read like a health report that first translates the hope of re-covery, summarizes slight improvements followed by relapses, and finally confirms the failure of therapy. Nietzsche returns to the North with his eye pains and his headaches, with the anguish of having to resume teaching at Basel, and the restlessness to devote himself to his philosophical calling. In Sorrento, his deepest self had begun to speak again. It was all the more difficult, now, to silence it, to stifle with the resumption of old professorial tasks this voice that spoke of freedom of the spirit and love of travel, this "self, old and always young" that aspired to new experiences, to new ideas, and to new paths. Should he have followed the sirens of free thought or remained a Wagnerian propagandist and a professor of philology at Basel? But which of these was the real siren? Which one truly diverted the traveler Odysseus from his path?

On April 10, accompanied to Naples by Malwida, Brenner and Rée had begun the journey back North after a sad farewell to their companions. Now the Villa Rubinacci had become much too quiet and empty, as Nietzsche de-scribes to Rée:

Until Friday, I remained alone at the Villa Rubinacci. Finally, Miss von Mey-senbug came back. Several days confined to bed, constantly *ill*, until today. Nothing is more desolate than your room without Rée. We exchange many words and silences concerning the absentee: yesterday, we decided that only your "appearance" had fled. In the evening, we play nine men's morris. No reading, Seydlitz is in bed; we have become the "charitable nurse" to one another, insofar as we take turns lying in bed. Dearest friend, how much I owe to you! I must never lose you! In deepest faithfulness, Your F. N.[1]

Alone with Malwida and Trina, Nietzsche begins to think again of his future. Half joking, he announces to his sister that he has resolved to abandon his professorship at Basel and to marry a good, *but* rich woman:

There is nothing more serene than your letter, dearest sister, which, on all possible fronts, hit the nail on the head. I am feeling so poorly! In fourteen days, I spent six in bed with six major attacks, the last of which sent me into total despair. When I got up, Miss von Meysenbug went to bed for three days because of her rheumatism. In the depths of our misery, we laughed a great deal when I read her selected passages from your letter. The plan that, in Miss von Meysenbug's opinion, should be regarded as unalterable and whose execution you must help with, is as follows. We have become convinced that my university existence at Basel cannot continue in the long term, that I could only push through it at the expense of my more important projects and, at the very least, at the total sacrifice of my health. True, I will have to spend next winter in these circumstances, but by Easter 1878, it must be brought to an end, provided the other combination succeeds, that is, my marriage to a suitable, though necessarily wealthy woman. "Good, *but* rich," as Miss von Meysenbug said, and that "but" made us laugh a great deal. With this wife, I would then go and live in Rome for the next few years, a place which is perfectly suited to my health, society, and my studies alike. This project would need to be inaugurated this summer in Switzerland, so that I would be married in time for my return to Basel in the fall. Various "entities" are invited to come to Switzerland; several names are entirely unknown to you, such as Elise Bülow from Berlin and Elisabeth Brandes from Hannover. As far as spiritual qualities are concerned, I think that Nathalie Herzen is the best qualified. You are very well acquainted with the idealization of little Köckert from Geneva! Praise, honor, and glory! But all of this is still precarious—and the fortune?[2]

With these plans for a radical change to his existence on his mind, Nietzsche prepares to abandon Sorrento, where the heat has become nearly unbearable to him. So he writes to his faithful friend Franz Overbeck in Basel on the day before his departure:

My health is ever worse, to such a degree that I must depart as soon as possible—I am bedridden every three days. Tomorrow, I am leaving by boat; I want to try a cure in Pfäfers, near Ragaz. [. . .] It is not to be *thought* that I will recommence my courses this fall: therefore! Please help me a little and advise me to whom (and with what title) I should make my *demission* request. This remains, for now, *your* secret; the decision was very difficult for me, but Miss von Meysenbug maintains that it is absolutely imperative. I must expect to live with my suffering for a long time to come, perhaps years. I cannot help but afflict you with this.[3]

Nietzsche thus leaves Sorrento on May 7, 1877, despite Malwida's strong advice to the contrary. Reinhart von Seydlitz and his wife accompany him to Naples, where the boat to Genoa is waiting. In a little diary that his sister had given him, we find a concise description of the journey:

May 8. Departure from Sorrento. *Mare molto cattivo*. May 10. Journey to Hell on the ship Ancona. May 11. Brignole (van Dyck), on foot again. May 12. 7:30, to Milan—12.90 *lire*—12.10 *lire*—Milan at 6 o'clock—4 *lire* 20 Chiasso 8 o'clock—Lugano 8:58. May 13. Flügge, manager of the central bureau at the Rostock post office. May 15. Dr. Dormann from Mayfield.—Pfäfers July–September: 1 franc breakfast—2.50 fr lunch—2–3 fr room—1 fr bath—Evening—8 centimes—without wine. May 23–24. Miss von Meysenbug tells me to wear my black fez.[4]

And in a long letter of May 13, we can follow the account of the journey as the philosopher tells it to his friends:

After long contemplation, I have come to the conclusion that although a postcard is lighter than a letter, it does not travel any faster, and so you must now resign yourself to a long narrative of my Odyssean wanderings up until now. Human misery during a sea voyage is terrible and at the same time ridiculous, in truth, just as my headaches sometimes seem ridiculous to me, when the body is such a flourishing thing—in short, today I am in the mood of the "cheerful invalid" again, whereas on the ship, I had only the blackest thoughts and, considering suicide, my only doubt was knowing where the sea was deepest so that I wouldn't be fished out right away and have to pay my rescuers an awful mass of gold out of gratitude. I was, moreover, at the worst stage of my seasickness at the time when I was hit by gastric pains accompanied by a headache: it was a "memory of half-forgotten times." To this was added the discomfort of needing to change positions three to eight times a minute, both by day and by night, and then having the odors and conversations of a feasting society in close proximity, which are immeasurably nauseating. At the port of Livorno, it was night and raining, and yet I wanted to get off the ship, but the captain's cold-blooded promises held me aboard. Inside the ship, everything rolled here and there with a great noise, pots and pans leapt about and came to life, children screamed, the storm howled; eternal wakefulness was my lot, the poet would say. The debarkation came with new sorrows; while entirely overcome by my dreadful headache, I had kept my strongest glasses on my nose for hours and distrusted everyone. Customs went tolerably well, but I forgot the essential thing, that is, to register my luggage for the railroad. Then we began the journey to the fabulous Hôtel National, with two scoundrels in the coachman's box who wanted with all their might to drop me off in a shabby inn; my luggage was constantly in different hands and there was always some man panting with my suitcase in front of me. Twice, I became furious and intimidated the coachman—the other one ran away. Do *you* know how I finally arrived at the Hôtel de Londres? I myself have no idea, but in the end it was *good*, only the entrance was awful, because there was an enormous crowd of criminals who wanted to be paid. I then went straight to bed, terribly languishing. On Friday, in the gloomy, rainy weather, I plucked up my courage at noon and went to the gallery of the Palazzo Brignole and, astonishingly, it was the sight of the family portraits that uplifted and inspired me; a Brignole on horseback, and in this powerful charger's *eye* lay all the pride of this family—that is what my depressed humanity needed! Personally, I esteem van Dyck and Rubens higher than all painters in the world. The other paintings left me cold, except for a dying Cleopatra by Guercino.

And so I came back to life, and spent the rest of the day sitting *quietly* and *spiritedly* in my hotel. The next day brought another exhilaration. I spent the whole journey from Genoa to Milan with a very nice young ballerina from a Milanese theater; Camilla *era molto simpathica* [*sic*], oh you should have heard my Italian! If I were a pasha, I would have taken her to Pfäfers with me, where, refusing my intellectual occupations, she could have danced something for me. I am still angry with myself from time to time for not having spent at least a couple of days with her in Milan. Now I was nearing Switzerland and for the first stretch, I took the Gotthard railway, which was recently finished, from Como to Lugano. But how did I come to Lugano? In truth I had no desire to, but here I am. As I crossed the Swiss border in the heavy rain, there was a single flash of lightning and a loud thunderclap. I took this as a good omen and I don't wish to conceal the fact that the closer I came to the mountains, the better I felt. In Chiasso, my luggage was sent off on two different trains, it was a frightful confusion, and on top of that, customs. Even my two umbrellas took opposite routes. Then, a nice luggage carrier came to help me and it was the first time I heard Swiss German spoken; you must know that I heard it with a certain emotion, and I realized suddenly that I much prefer to live among Swiss Germans than among Germans. The man looked after me so well, he was so fatherly, running here and there—all fathers are somewhat clumsy—that in the end I had all of my luggage again and resumed my journey to Lugano. The car of the Hôtel du Parc awaited me and here a true exaltation arose in me, everything is so perfect that I would even say it is the best hotel in the world. I have made the acquaintance of a rural nobleman from Mecklenburg, *that* is certainly a type of German I can get along with; in the evening I watched an improvised ball of the most harmless sort, nothing but English people, it was all so comical. After which I slept deeply and well for the first time; and this morning I can see all of my beloved mountains before me, all the mountains of my memory. It has been raining here for eight days. Today at the post office I will inquire about the state of the Alpine passes.

Now the thought has suddenly come to me that it has been years since I wrote such a long letter and that you will not even be able to read it.[5]

See, then, in the *fact of this letter* a sign of my improvement. [. . .] I think of you with heartfelt affection many times an hour; I've been given the gift of maternal love, and I will never forget it. [. . .] Farewell! Please remain for me what you have been and I will feel much more protected and secure; for sometimes I am so overcome with the feeling of solitude that I want to scream. Your grateful and devoted Friedrich Nietzsche. Third narrative of Odysseus.[6]

In response to that letter sent to Malwida, Reinhart von Seydlitz writes to Nietzsche from Sorrento, enclosing an amusing little drawing in his letter:

Without any mockery, dear friend, I wish you bright, joyous courage and happiness with all my heart. We are all delighted by the cheerful mood that came laughing to us from your letter.

I am astounded to hear how the trip to the Alps smiled on you. It's wonderful at the Hôtel du Parc; I consider it an excellent hotel.

Enough for today, you reckless philosopher, and a warm salutation from your amazed and overjoyed friend, Rinaldo.[7]

Malwida also responded to Nietzsche, congratulating him on having recovered his good spirits:

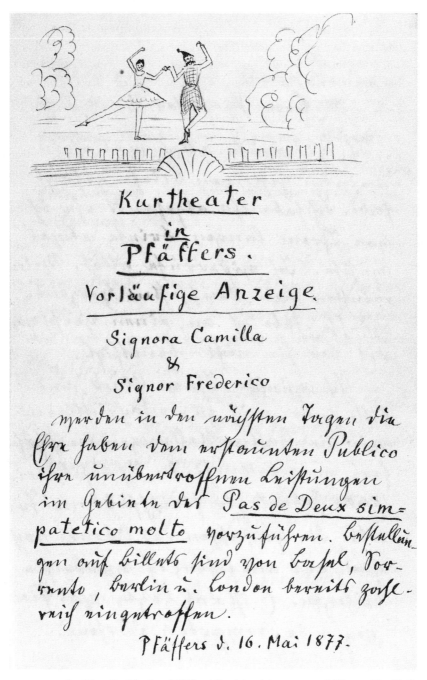

FIGURE 28: *"Curative Theater of Pfäffers | Provisional Announcement | Signora Camilla &
Signor Frederico | will have the honor in the coming days to present to the astounded publico*
[*sic*] their unrivaled performances in the domain of *Pas de Deux simpatetico molto* [*sic*]. Numerous
ticket reservations have already arrived from Basel, Sorrento, Berlin, and London. / Pfäffers, May
16, 1877." Camilla e Frederico. Von Seydlitz to Nietzsche, GSA 71/BW211. KGW II/6/1, 556-557.

Dear friend, how good it was that your letter from Lugano followed the sorrowful postcards from Genoa so quickly! You had plunged me into the deepest unrest about you—but Calypso, who so encouraged Odysseus in his wanderings, reassured me a great deal. In the future, if you think of suicide again, I will shout to you: *Ché! Camilla è molto simpatica* and then you must regain your calm and have *coraggio* and *pazienza*. Yesterday, Seydlitz showed me a very pretty illustration of the event, which will surely amuse you very much.[8]

But the philosopher's manuscripts tell another story, to which Nietzsche does not allude at all in the letter to his friends. Mazzino Montinari wrote: "Nietzsche's life is in his thoughts, in his books. Nietzsche is an example of a rare mental concentration, of cruel and continual exertion of the intellect, of internalization and sublimation of personal experiences from the most exceptional to the most banal, of reduction of what is communally called 'life' to 'spirit,' where this word is understood in the German sense of 'Geist,' which is understanding-intelligence, also interiority or spirituality (but not mysticism or *Seele*, soul)."[9] If Nietzsche's life is in his thoughts, the true biographical event that distills the philosophical meaning of this first journey South is contained in a few lines written in pencil in one of the notebooks that he had with him during the sea crossing. Even if in Sorrento he had been inclined toward the acceptance of life and retained in his memory the words of Spinoza quoted in the introduction ("The free man thinks of nothing less than death, and his knowledge is not a meditation on death but on life"), he still had a long path to travel. The Sorrento papers that he carries with him in his suitcase and the plan for a new book, still untitled, constitute a promise of freedom, but also an imposing task. Will he ever find the strength and the courage to write it and publish it? Would it not be simpler to give up entirely? A sea storm and a bad crossing are enough to arouse doubt in him about the value of life and when, at dawn, the lights of the port at Genoa emerge, words much darker than those he sent to his friends come to him:

> Desire for death, like the one who, being seasick and seeing the port's lights late at night, desires land.

This thought appears in a notebook written on land at Genoa, probably the following day, March 11th, and on the same page there is another brief note:

> Peal of bells in the evening in Genoa—melancholy, chilling, childlike. Plato: nothing mortal is worthy of great seriousness.[10]

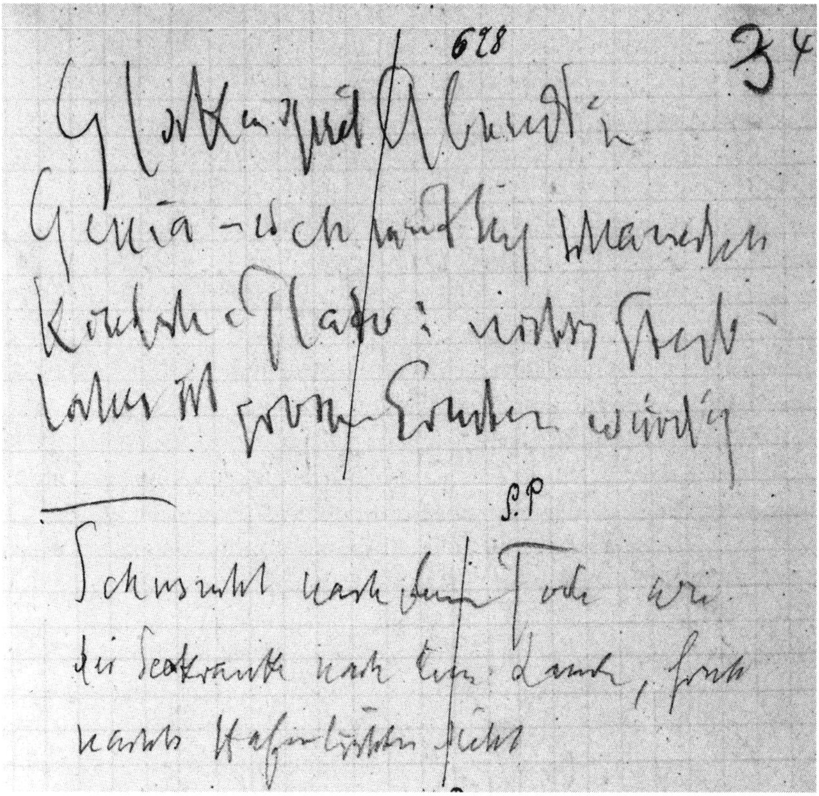

FIGURE 29 : Nietzsche, notebook N II 2, page 4. GSA 71/174.

Walking through the streets of Genoa at twilight, Nietzsche had heard the peal of the bells coming from the top of a tower. In one instant, the memories of a pastor's son, the philologist's erudition, and the philosopher's reflection merge into an experience of thought that overwhelms and deeply moves him. The page of this notebook holds its first written trace.

EPIPHANIES

The bells of Genoa are a Nietzschean epiphany. In Greek culture, epiphany meant the manifestation (ἐπιφάνεια) of a divinity, or more precisely the signs through which an invisible divinity indicated its presence: visions, dreams, miracles. In the Christian world, the term is used once again, from the third century on, to designate the commemorative celebration of the principal manifestations of Jesus Christ's divinity (baptism, adoration of the Magi, first miracle), later confining itself, in the occidental Church and in popular tradition, to designating exclusively the coming of the Magi. In the contemporary world, James Joyce used the term epiphany in a particular sense to refer to these moments of sudden intuition where the meaning of an object is revealed to the knowing subject or when an event revives a buried memory in remembrance that comes to show itself in all its details and with all the emotions that are tied to it. In the evolution of his poetics and of his literary projects, the concept of the epiphany used by Joyce underwent various modifications and definitions. In a collection of epiphanies from 1900, they are presented in the form of very short, autonomous dramatic or narrative compositions, staging or recalling a significant moment in his life wherein "the spirit of beauty had folded him round like a mantle."[11] Later, in his first attempt at a novel (*Stephen Hero*, 1904), he includes a theoretical explanation of the concept of the epiphany:

> By an epiphany [Stephen] meant a sudden spiritual manifestation, whether in the vulgarity of speech or of gesture or in a memorable phase of the mind itself. He believed that it was for the man of letters to record these epiphanies with extreme care, seeing that they themselves are the most delicate and evanescent of moments. He told Cranly that the clock of the Ballast Office was capable of an epiphany. [. . .] "What?" "Imagine my glimpses at that clock as the gropings of a spiritual eye which seeks to adjust its vision to an exact focus. The moment the focus is reached the object is epiphanised. It is just in this epiphany that I find the third, the supreme quality of beauty."[12]

The third quality of beauty refers to Thomas Aquinas's aesthetic doctrine: *Ad pulchritudinem, tria requiruntur: integritas, consonantia, claritas* ("There are three things required for beauty: wholeness, harmony, radiance"):

> For a long time I couldn't make out what Aquinas meant. He uses a figurative word (a very unusual thing for him) but I have solved it. *Claritas* is *quidditas*. After the analysis which discovers the second quality the mind makes the only logically possible synthesis and discovers the third quality. This is the moment which I call epiphany. First we recognize that the object is *one* integral thing, then we recognize that it is an organised composite structure, a *thing* in fact: finally, when the relation of the parts is exquisite, when the parts are adjusted to the special point, we recognize that it is *that* thing which it is. Its soul, its whatness, leaps to us from the vestment of its appearance. The soul of the commonest object, the structure of which is so adjusted, seems to us radiant. The object achieves its epiphany.[13]

Rather than borrowing from a scholastic conception, the concept of the epiphany reflected, in fact, the concluding words of Walter Pater's studies on *The Renaissance*, with their praise of the esthete seeking to enjoy each moment of perfection and to render the fugitive instant absolute. He inserted himself into an aesthetics of the instant that would blossom in the first years of the twentieth century through such authors as Marcel Proust, D. H. Lawrence, Virginia Woolf, and T. S. Eliot. If the concept had come from Pater in the context of the end of romanticism and the beginning of symbolism, Joyce had found the term epiphany in D'Annunzio's *The Flame*, whose first chapter is titled "Epiphany of Fire."[14]

When rewriting his novel under the new title *A Portrait of the Artist as a Young Man*, although he conserves the equivalence between *caritas* and *quidditas*, Joyce does not use the term epiphany. To convey the coloration of this mysterious instant, he instead uses two comparisons, one taken from Shelley and one from Galvani.[15] Beginning in 1904, Joyce no longer conceives of epiphanies as autonomous compositions but as elements of construction, simple notes which in 1909 will be classified in an alphabetical list, organized by subject, and prepared to be used in the *Portrait* and later in *Ulysses*. In the third chapter of *Ulysses*, as he walks and reflects upon the beach of Sandymount, Stephen pokes fun at the epiphanies of his youth: "Remember your epiphanies written on green oval leaves, deeply deep, copies to be sent if you died to all the great libraries in the world, including Alexandria?"[16] *Finnegans Wake* marks a return to the epiphany, projected onto the scale of the entire work, itself become a single and "gigantic epiphany of human language" that uses the dislocation of locution, or "dislocution," to produce a detachment and allow for a new and surprised gaze to be cast, not so much on things, but on words. The novel ends with the apocalypse of the epiphany, or the *Apophanype*. In the last and final book, the Apocalypse of Joyce's New Testament, he writes: "Wrhps, that wind out of norewere! As on the night of the Apophanypes!"[17]

Nietzsche's epiphanies have nothing to do with the Christian tradition, the poetics of the instant, or Joyce's epiphanies. We have sketched this short history of several uses of the word epiphany to make a very clear distinction between the meaning we are giving it and its past uses. Nietzsche did not use the term epiphany in his works, but we will use it as a critical concept in order to understand certain characteristics of the genesis and structure of his philosophical writing. If he did not use the word, Nietzsche was certainly aware that our existence is measured by moments of intense significance and that these moments represent the most meaningful modulations in the symphony of life:

Of the hour-hand of life. —Life consists of rare individual moments of the highest significance and countless intervals in which at best the phantoms of those moments hover about us. Love, spring, a beautiful melody, the mountains, the moon, the sea—they all speak truly to our heart only once: if they ever do in fact truly find speech. For many people never experience these moments at all but are themselves intervals and pauses in the symphony of real life.[18]

Sometimes, the trace of these epiphanies can be found in the philosopher's notebooks. There are biographical epiphanies, as when Nietzsche remembers the first time when, as a child, near a stream in Plauen, he saw butterflies in the spring sunlight; or when, in a tiny diary, he notes a series of *Memorabilia* that tell of the happy days of his life, reviving the feeling of lost childhood or evoking the strict voice of his father.[19] Biographical epiphanies are rare in Nietzsche's writings. The philosopher felt "as though shot by the curare arrow of knowledge" and the most important events of his life were, in truth, his own thoughts.[20] Authentic Nietzschean epiphanies thus speak of philosophy; they are epiphanies of knowledge, mental short-circuits which, in a spark, resolve a philosophical problem or open new perspectives through the association of apparently remote concepts. Certain epiphanies are particularly important because they announce a turning point, signal a jolt in the process of reflection, and lend acceleration to Nietzsche's already very swift thinking. Nietzsche's philosophical epiphanies can thus be used as a heuristic instrument within a genetic perspective, as the signal of a deep emotive disturbance brought on by the birth of a new cognitive scenario. Following these epiphanies will help us to discover the movement, sometimes subterranean, of Nietzsche's thought and to understand its deeper transformations. Not all of the epiphanies mark a turning point, but every metamorphosis in Nietzsche's philosophy is preceded or accompanied by an epiphany.[21]

But what are the status and the form of the epiphany in Nietzsche's philosophy? First of all, we must specify that Nietzschean epiphanies do not establish any sort of "vertical" relationship. What appears to the subject is not a transcendent quality in the object, its essence, its *quidditas*, not even its deeper meaning. In Nietzschean ontology, essences do not exist, nor do the originary meanings of things; the objects of our world are forms in continual movement and, even during periods of relative stability, their meaning changes constantly: "The form is fluid, but the 'meaning' is even more so."[22] Thus, from an epistemological perspective, Nietzschean epiphanies are not instants of mystical illumination, expressions of a nonrational knowledge where an ontologically different dimension manifests, to which the inspired subject would have a privileged access. They are, on the contrary, the concentration or the condensation of multiple rational fields of knowledge. Nietzschean epiphanies are moments in which all the fertile semantic wealth of an event, an object, or a concept appears to the philosopher unexpectedly.

In our view, they display three characteristics. In the first place, they are a *crossroads of meaning* because, far from establishing a vertical relationship with essences, they are the meeting point of a horizontal relationship between lines of thought that originate in different contexts. They are instants in which a confluence appears to the subject between philosophical theories, personal experiences, or literary images that preoccupy him for a certain time in a single mental figure that sums them up perfectly. In the second place, if epiphanies have no transcendence, they do have a depth, a *historical depth.* Accompanying the semantic lines that arise from the present state of his reflection, the many stratifications of meaning that constitute the history of the object are also made manifest to the philosopher's mind, i.e., the connotations which have been given to the object through literature, art, philosophy, or simple linguistic use (metaphors, metonymies). And finally, the philosopher has the intuition of the *semantic potentiality* of the epiphanic event. The third important characteristic of Nietzschean epiphanies, indeed, is that they are instruments for the production of meaning. In the moment of the epiphany, the philosopher understands that he can unite and merge together various elements of a cultural tradition into a single image that becomes the bearer, and more importantly, the generative force of meaning—like a crucible that has already collected numerous significations and is still vast and malleable enough to allow for the creation of a new meaning to be compounded with the preexisting strata, modifying the direction of tradition, sometimes by reversing or parodying it. To summarize: in the moment of the epiphany, the subject has the intuition of the object's capacity to become the symbol of a certain worldview, thanks to a convergence of multiple significations that are unexpectedly and coherently condensed into an image. Moreover, he becomes aware that the object, through a whole literary, philosophical, artistic tradition, has been endowed with different supplies of meaning that make up, from this point forward, no longer its *quidditas* but its historical depth. And finally, along with the fabric of preexisting connotations, the vitality and semantic potentiality of the epiphanic image appear to the philosopher, which make possible the image's reemployment and reinterpretation in a new philosophical context.

On the basis of these observations, we can see how different the Nietzschean epiphany is from that of Joyce. There is a difference of *status*, because the Nietzschean epiphany is equidistant from the *quidditas* of *Dedalus* and the commonplaces of *Ulysses*: it does not express the essence of the object and possesses a more complex semantic value than a series of commonplaces. Additionally, we notice certain differences in *function*. For the writer, the epiphany is a stopping point before the image that reveals the "luminous silent stasis of esthetic pleasure,"[23] while for the philosopher, the epiphany is a drive for a new movement in thought. For Joyce, the epiphany is a particular stylistic strategy that is finalized in the construction of the literary text. For Nietzsche, on the contrary, the epiphany is a private experience that gives rise to a new cognitive scenario, which, however, is not necessarily used afterward in the writing of the philosophical text. When it is used, the text does not so much contain the initial epiphanic moment but the knowledge and the philosophical contents that have been drawn from it. Consequently, Nietzschean epiphanies often remain confined to the pages of his notebooks and do not appear as such in the published text. The epiphany is an illuminating signal that can be detected in the philosopher's papers and reveals to us the importance of an image or a philosophical theme. Following the trace of these epiphanies thus allows us to reconstruct the genesis of the Nietzschean text and to better understand the evolutions of his philosophy and the importance of certain fundamental concepts, which we will then recover, often divested of the epiphanic aspect, published in the form of pure philosophical concepts. The epiphany is an interpretive instrument that serves to shed light on the movement of the Nietzschean text.

THE VALUE OF HUMAN THINGS

Let us return, now, to the epiphany of Genoa to analyze the elements that compose it.

> *Glockenspiel Abends in Genua—wehmütig schauerlich kindisch. Plato: nichts Sterbliches ist grossen Ernstes würdig.*
> Peal of bells in the evening in Genoa—melancholy, chilling, childlike. Plato: nothing mortal is worthy of great seriousness.

At least three semantic levels combine in this sudden illumination: a biographical level, a literary level, and a more strictly philosophical level. At the biographical level, the peal of the bells that toll the hours of the day and accompany religious services had caused a stream of memories to resurface from the depths of Nietzsche's soul—memories of a pastor's son from the small village of Röcken ("Like a plant, I was born near the cemetery, like a man, in a presbytery").[24] In his autobiographies and in the poems of his youth, we find numerous traces of the deep impression that the peal of bells produced in him, often evoked in words similar to those of the Genoa epiphany. In 1858, at the age of fourteen, Nietzsche describes the happy time of his childhood in the village of Röcken; the steeple and carillon constitute the visual and aural representation of this period, associated as they are with the image of his father and his role in the community. These old and deep memories explain why, in the peal of the bells, Nietzsche hears all the *melancholy* (one of the words that we found in the note on the bells) of lost childhood: "What springs to mind before all else is its steeple covered over in moss. I still clearly remember a time when I traveled from Lützen to Röcken with my beloved father, and how, midway, we heard the solemn chimes of the Easter services. This sound often rings out in me, and melancholy brings me back at once to the distant and dear paternal home. How vivid the cemetery is in my memory! How many times I've wondered, upon seeing the old, old tombstones, about the caskets and the black crêpe, about the ancient epitaphs and the sepulchers!"[25] Unfortunately, hardly a year after this happy journey, the bells resounded again to accompany the mortal corpse of Nietzsche's father. This sound, which represented the joy of childhood, home, family, would from then on be associated with the *horror* of death and the separation from places dear to his heart: "Finally, after a long time, the horrible took place: my father died. Still today, this thought touches me deeply and painfully"; "On August second, they entrusted my beloved father's mortal corpse to the earth. The town hall had prepared the tomb. The ceremony began at one in the afternoon, all the bells resounding. Oh, never will their harrowing pealing fade from my aural memory"; "How the funeral choked me! The harrowing sound of the death knell made me shiver to the marrow of my bones. At first, I felt orphaned and abandoned, I understood that I had lost the father I loved. [. . .] The time had come for us to leave our dear home. I still remember very precisely the last day and the last night there. In the evening, I played once more with a group of children, without forgetting for a single instant that it was for the last time. And then, to them as well as all the places that had become so dear to me, I said farewell. The evening bell resounded melancholically above the fields. A half-darkness spread over our village, the moon had risen, and we watched its pale glow above."[26] In the letters and poems of this period, we also find this association between the sound of bells and death. For example, in a poem of 1859 titled "Bell of the Vespers": "The vespers ring out softly beyond the fields. They tell my heart that no one in the world ever finds his blessed country: that once we leave the earth we return to the earth. This echo of the bells gives birth to a thought in me: we are all on the way to eternity."[27]

FIGURE 30 : The bell tower of the village of Röcken. Private collection.

At the age of sixteen, as a student at the prestigious school of Pforta, Nietzsche writes to his mother on the Day of the Dead: "Yesterday at 6 o'clock, at the chiming of the bells, I thought very deeply of you and of the hours we have spent together through the years. In the evening, the service for the dead was sung and the lives were read of the students of Pforta who came before us and are deceased."[28] Two years later, he composes a poem titled "The Night before the Day of the Dead," where the peal of bells in the wintry night reawakens in him the memory, slumbering in the depths of his heart, of those close to him who have died. At the sound of the bells, the dead awake and invite the young man to join them in their long, frozen sleep.[29] From a biographical point of view, therefore, the meaning of bells is *melancholy* and *childlike* because the world of lost childhood resounds in him; and it is *chilling* because it is associated with the thought of death. The bells pierce the heart of the one who retains the memory of the dead.

This personal experience is progressively filtered through a whole series of literary reminiscences. As it is well known, the death knell tolls in Schiller's famous "Song of the Bell": "From the cathedral, / heavy and glum / tolls the bell / a funereal dirge. / Its mournful strokes accompany with seriousness / a pilgrim on his final journey."[30] And Goethe, in his "Epilogue to Schiller's 'The Song of the Bell,'" had renewed this motif to remind us of the death of his friend: "I hear horrible strokes of midnight, / mournful sounds rising, heavy and glum. / Is it possible? Is it truly for our friend [. . .]?"[31] When he reads Byron's *The Two Foscari* in 1861, Nietzsche is struck by the figure of the old doge who dies unexpectedly upon hearing the bells of San Marco announcing the election of his successor. Two years later, Nietzsche uses this motif once again in a poem devoted to the fiftieth anniversary of the battle of Leipzig to express Napoleon's anxiety when, hearing the bells toll, he thinks, like the old doge, of the end of his political parabola and of death: "From Leipzig the bells ring out this instant, / a funeral song for the Day of the Dead [. . .] Do you hear it, my generals? / The heart of a stricken doge was broken / one day by the fault of this proud carillon! / My heart too hears a shattering song— / will it have to break? Give me counsel!"[32] In his letters on the French theater, Heinrich Heine had traced the sonorous image of death using the same terms as those of the Nietzschean epiphany: "In Autumn the sound of the bells is even more serious [*ernster*], even more frightening [*schauerlicher*], and one believes that he hears the voice of a ghost. Particularly during a funeral, the pealing of the bells sounds in an ineffably melancholy [*wehmütigen*] way; at each stroke, sick yellow leaves fall from the tree, and this musical fall of the leaves, this sonorous image of death [*Sterbens*] once filled me with such an overpowering mourning that I began to cry like a child."[33] The allusion to the seriousness, *Ernst*, of the pealing of bells was also present in Schiller's lines quoted above, and it returns in the concluding stanzas where the bell, from the top of the cathedral tower, reminds us of the vanity of human things compared to the seriousness and the eternity of heavenly things: "High above base earthly life / She must float in the azure firmament, / Sister of thunder / [. . .] That only to serious and eternal things / Her metallic voice be dedicated / [. . .] And as the powerful sound that rings out from her / Fades and vanishes to our ear / So teaches the bell that nothing persists / That everything earthly is mortal."[34] In these illustrious examples, Nietzsche finds a common vocabulary and a literary topos that allow him to express, in a more general and communal way, an experience that was originally limited to the individual sphere.

The third element confers on the epiphany its more strictly philosophical meaning, drawing together the biographical and literary image of the bell, the sonorous symbol of death and of the fragility of human things, with the devalorization of existence expressed in the words of Plato. In the seventh book of his last dialogue, *The Laws*, Plato speaks of the education of the youth and proposes a series of lessons to make the bodies and souls of the young both beautiful and strong. These are practices, uses, and habits that form a corpus of unwritten laws and represent the cohesive element of any society. Plato describes the games, the punishments, the types of gymnastics and music, distinguishing those that are better suited to boys and to girls. Then, feeling the weight of all this work of the minute regulation of something that in itself is not worthy of so much trouble, he indulges himself in a more general reflection and writes: "In truth, human affairs are not worthy of being treated with great seriousness, and yet we must take them seriously, although it is unfortunate." He then explains himself: "I say that one must treat serious things with seriousness, and not things that are not serious. The divine is by nature worthy of serious and blessed things, while man, as we said before, is only a plaything constructed by the gods, and this attribute is truly what is best in him. Thus all men and women must live according to their nature and play the most beautiful games."[35] Plato expressed the same concept in a passage of *The Republic*, taken up again by Schopenhauer in his *Parerga and Paralipomena*: "Whoever, having penetrated the teachings of my philosophy, knows that our existence is a thing that should not be and that the supreme wisdom consists in denying and rejecting it, he will not found great hopes on any thing or situation, will pursue nothing with passion, and will not raise complaint against any disappointment, but he will recognize the truth of Plato's words (*Rep.* X, 604): οὔτε τι τῶν ἀνθρωπίνων ἄξιον ὂν μεγάλης σπουδῆς."[36] Thanks to Albert Brenner's testimony, we know that in Sorrento, in December 1876, during the evenings of communal reading, the little community had read Plato's *Laws*.[37] And Plato's words, "All that is human is not worthy of great seriousness" can also be found, isolated and enigmatic, written in a Sorrento notebook.[38] But already several months before traveling to Sorrento, while he was teaching a course at the university on the fundamental concepts of Platonic philosophy, Nietzsche had pondered the validity of his metaphysics of art in his personal notes: "If Plato were right! If man were a pretty plaything in the hands of the gods! [. . .] If existence were nothing other than an aesthetic phenomenon! Then the artist would not only be the most reasonable and the wisest man, and would be one man with the philosopher, but he would have an easy and carefree life and he could say in all good conscience, like Plato: human things are not worthy of great seriousness [*die menschlichen Dinge sind grossen Ernstes nicht werth*]."[39] If Plato were right . . . According to *The Birth of Tragedy*, Plato *was* right: man was a plaything in the hands of the gods, existence was justified only as an aesthetic phenomenon, and the artist was the supreme product of nature. And one could accept that human things were worth nothing, because, regardless, another dimension existed, the metaphysical dimension, and this justified life. But in this fragment of 1875, Plato is no longer right. The fragment ends by saying that art serves precisely to transfigure a life that has no value:

"Doesn't the existence of art demonstrate precisely that life is an anti-aesthetic phenomenon, wicked and serious? Let us pay attention once more to what a real thinker, Leopardi, says." The pessimism of Giacomo Leopardi is now, for Nietzsche, more profound than Plato's thought, because it is divested of transcendent illusions.[40] There is no metaphysical dimension that could save us from pessimism and allow us to take the lack of value of human things lightly. Nothing that is human has value, and the divine does not exist.

After Genoa, Nietzsche continues his sabbatical leave in the village of Rosenlauibad, in the Bernese Alps, where he brings only three books with him: *The Adventures of Tom Sawyer* by Mark Twain, *The Origin of the Moral Sensations* by Paul Rée, and Plato's *Laws*. For the philosopher lost in his thoughts, who awakes one Sunday morning in a small village of the Alps, the sound of the bells produces an effect of detachment, like something coming from very far off, like a fragment of antiquity and the remnants of a long-lost culture. And he jots down in his notebook: "In the morning church bells in the Bernese Alps—in honor of a crucified Jew who claimed to be the son of God." From this first impression, he will later draw aphorism 113 of *Things Human, All Too Human*: "*Christianity as antiquity.* — When on a Sunday morning we hear the bells ringing we ask ourselves: is it possible! this is going on because of a Jew crucified 2,000 years ago who said he was the son of God. The proof of such an assertion is lacking. —In the context of our age the Christian religion is certainly a piece of antiquity intruding out of distant ages past, and that the above-mentioned assertion is believed—while one is otherwise so rigorous in the testing of claims—is perhaps the most ancient piece of this inheritance. A God who begets children of a mortal woman; [. . .] someone who bids his disciples to drink his blood; prayers for miraculous interventions; sin perpetrated against a God atoned for by a God; fear of a Beyond to which death is the gateway; the figure of the Cross as a symbol in an age that no longer knows the meaning and shame of the Cross—how gruesomely all this is wafted to us, as if out of the grave of a primeval past! Can one believe that things of this sort are still believed in?"[41] If the bells of Genoa represented the horror of death and Plato's nihilism, in the bells of Rosenlauibad Nietzsche hears resounding the error of faith and the Platonism of the poor: Christianity.

Let us stop for a moment to draw up a preliminary assessment of the meaning of the Genoa epiphany. Nietzsche uses certain terms that, in more than their literal sense, also play the role of key words, of precise intertextual references. The philosopher expected a good reader, an erudite contemporary, in reading the word "bells," to hear the words of Byron, Goethe, Schiller, Heine, and, in reading his remarks on the absence of value of human things, to think of Plato,

Schopenhauer, Leopardi, and the Christian doctrine. In two sentences jotted down in pencil in his notebook, Nietzsche embeds the literary topos of the bells within the theme of the devalorization of existence contained in Plato's words and condenses them into a symbolic image with which he endows a precise philosophical meaning: the bell as an extreme symbol of pessimism, of nihilism, and of Christianity. And although it may not be strictly indispensable for understanding the text, we who come after him can also read therein a reference to Nietzsche's childhood and the death of his father, such as they are narrated in the poems and the autobiographical texts of his youth. We also have the capacity to follow the rewritings of these lines through Nietzsche's notebooks and hence try to understand not only how he composed this symbolic image but also the meaning that he intends to confer upon it. As we shall see, Nietzsche will reinforce the semantic field of this image even further in two ways: by placing it in a strategic position within the textual and conceptual architecture of his body of work and by putting it into play with other symbolic images.

CROSSED GENESES

Let us now try to follow the development of this epiphany and parse the process by which it grows rich in significations through its rewritings. In Rosenlauibad, carrying the memory of the literary tradition, Nietzsche seeks to reformulate the Genoa intuition in verse. This poetic rewriting is centered on three recurring adjectives (melancholy, chilling, childlike) and introduces a play on words between *Glockenspiel* and *Glockenernst*, "sound of bells" (literally "game of bells") and "seriousness of bells," but not yet with the reference to Plato.

> Childlike and chilling and melancholy
> I've often heard the melody of time
> see, is it her song I sing?
> hear, if the game of her carillon
> hasn't taken on a serious tone
> or if it doesn't ring out
> as if it came from the height of the tower of Genoa.
> Childlike and yet, alas, chilling
> Chilling and melancholy.[42]

Once he has returned to Basel, Nietzsche works on the writing of his new book and the epiphany of the bells mingles once again with words on the desire for death.

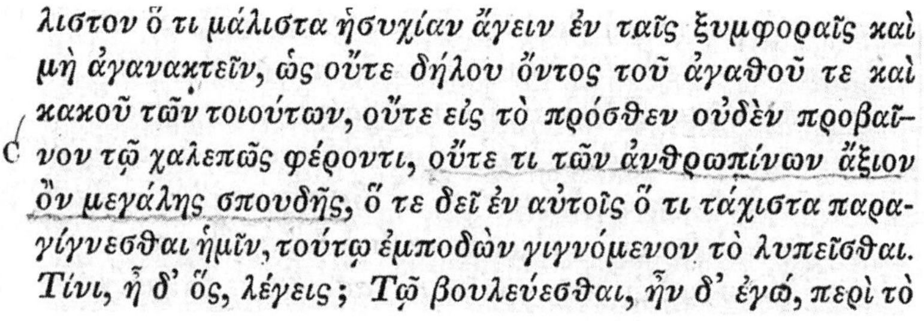

λιστον ὅ τι μάλιστα ἡσυχίαν ἄγειν ἐν ταῖς ξυμφοραῖς καὶ
μὴ ἀγανακτεῖν, ὡς οὔτε δήλου ὄντος τοῦ ἀγαθοῦ τε καὶ
κακοῦ τῶν τοιούτων, οὔτε εἰς τὸ πρόσθεν οὐδὲν προβαῖ-
νον τῷ χαλεπῶς φέροντι, οὔτε τι τῶν ἀνθρωπίνων ἄξιον
ὂν μεγάλης σπουδῆς, ὅ τε δεῖ ἐν αὐτοῖς ὅ τι τάχιστα παρα-
γίγνεσθαι ἡμῖν, τούτῳ ἐμποδὼν γιγνόμενον τὸ λυπεῖσθαι.
Τίνι, ἦ δ' ὅς, λέγεις; Τῷ βουλεύεσθαι, ἦν δ' ἐγώ, περὶ τὸ

FIGURE 31: Nietzsche's copy of Plato's *Republic* with the sentence on the value of human things underlined. Herzogin Anna Amalia Bibliothek, shelf mark C 63-b, 298.

The two notations that we read on the same page of the Sorrento notebook are recopied on a sheet of paper, number 222 of a group of loose sheets destined for *Things Human, All Too Human*; the one that speaks of the bells of Genoa is titled *Alles Menschliches insgesamt*, all that is human, and the one that speaks of suicide, *Sehnsucht nach dem Tode*, desire for death.

> *All that is human.* I heard one evening in Genoa a peal of bells coming from the steeple of a church: it was a thing so melancholy, chilling, childlike, that I experienced what Plato said: "nothing that is human is worthy of great seriousness."
> *Desire for death.* — As the one who is seasick watches, in the boat, from the first lights of dawn, the appearance of the coast, so one often longs for death— knowing that he can change neither the speed nor the direction of his boat.[43]

The most telling difference of this reformulation is the use of the term *Menschliches*; that which is human, in the place of the initial term *Sterbliches*, that which is mortal. This suggests that Nietzsche had revisited Plato's text. And perhaps it is precisely on this occasion that he underlined the words οὔτε τι τῶν ἀνθρωπίνων ἄξιον ὂν μεγάλης σπουδῆς in his copy of *The Republic*.[44]

In the course of the next genetic step, we note two important modifications. The aphorism on the bells is retranscribed with several changes. The aphorism on suicide disappears: it will be neither transcribed nor published by Nietzsche. Why? Let us first look at the modifications. Nietzsche added a point, the adversative *trotzdem* (nonetheless, however, yet), which becomes the very title of the aphorism.

> *Yet.* — In Genoa at the time of evening twilight I heard a long peal of bells coming from a tower: it seemed it would never stop, resounding as though it

could never have enough of itself over the noise of the streets out into the evening sky and the sea breeze, so chilling, at the same time so childlike, infinitely melancholy. Then it reminded me of the words of Plato and suddenly I felt them in my heart: *Nothing human is worthy of great seriousness; and yet——*[45]

Instead of limiting himself to deeply experiencing and expressing all the anguish of the devalorization of the world, of error, of death, the anguish of the human condition in the face of the vision of atemporal eternity as imagined by Plato, by Christianity, and through them by a whole philosophical tradition, Nietzsche now takes up the challenge. He adds a *trotzdem*: nothing has value, all is in vain, and yet . . . Taking up the challenge also means giving up on suicide, and this explains why the genesis of the aphorism on the nostalgia for death was interrupted at this precise moment. The genetic development of the other aphorism, on the other hand, continues with the introduction of a final textual and structural modification that is very telling. Indeed, in the manuscript sent to the typographer, this aphorism on the vanity of human things will be titled *Epilogue* and placed on the last page of a book that—not by chance—will be called *Menschliches, Allzumenschliches, Things Human, All Too Human.*[46] Thus, the aphorism and the book on human things end with an adversative that remains in suspense and that is followed by two *Gedankenstriche*, two em dashes. In Nietzsche's writing, this typographical character often corresponds to a strategy of reticence that serves to distinguish the most superficial contents of the thought from the most profound, and that invites the reader to consider the aphorism more deeply.

It thus has a double effect: "on one hand it draws the reasoning into the foreground, announcing that a sudden turn will take place; on the other hand it 'pushes it back,' forcing the reader to return to what he has just read, pondering it and reinterpreting it in light of new elements."[47] The two dashes placed at the end of the last aphorism, then, invite us to reread not only the aphorism itself, but also the entire book in light of the bells of nihilism, inserting it into a context of thought that goes back to Plato and to the whole pessimist tradition, and considering that nonetheless, *trotzdem*, there must be a way to give value to human things. *Things Human, All Too Human* addresses precisely this. Nietzsche takes a stance against Plato, against pessimism, and proposes the outlines of another vision: chemistry of ideas and feelings, confidence in history and science, Epicurism, innocence in becoming, reevaluation of the nearest things . . .[48]

The saga of the genesis of the aphorism on the Genoa bells is not yet over. During the correction of the draft, Nietzsche adds ten aphorisms before the

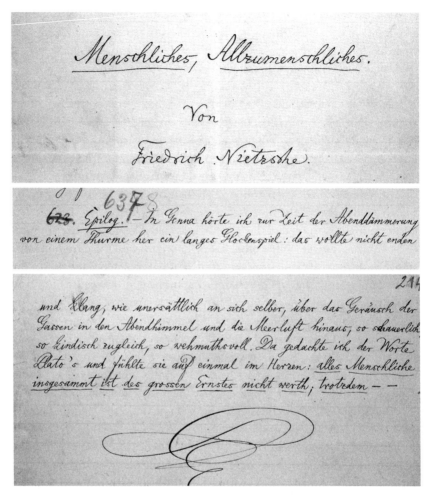

F I G U R E 3 2 : Manuscript of *Things Human, All Too Human* sent to printer, title page and final aphorism. GSA 71/14,1 and 71/14,9.

epilogue which, in the second draft, changes from number 628 to number 638 (cf. figure 33). But afterward, at the last minute, Nietzsche exchanges aphorism 638 with aphorism 628, and the aphorism on the bells thus loses its position at the end. Consequently, Nietzsche also changes the title of the aphorism which, from *Epilog* becomes *Spiel und Ernst, Play and Seriousness*—an allusion to the fact that a *Glockenspiel*, a "play of bells" resounds in the aphorism—and then, continuing the play on words, Nietzsche finds the definitive title: *Ernst im Spiele, Seriousness in Play.* Must we conclude that the echo effect between the

— 377 —

von Meinung zu Meinung, durch den Wechsel aller
Parteien, als edle Verräther aller Dinge, die überhaupt
verrathen werden — und dennoch ohne ein Gefühl von
Schuld.

638.

Epilog. — In Genua hörte ich zur Zeit der Abend-
dämmerung von einem Thurme her ein langes Glockenspiel: das wollte nicht enden und klang, wie unersättlich
an sich selber, über das Geräusch der Gassen in den
Abendhimmel und die Meerluft hinaus, so schauerlich,
so kindisch zugleich, so wehmuthsvoll. Da gedachte ich
der Worte Plato's und fühlte sie auf einmal im Herzen:
alles Menschliche insgesammt ist des grossen
Ernstes nicht werth; trotzdem — —

FIGURE 33: Proof of the final aphorism of *Things Human, All Too Human*. Herzogin Anna Amalia Bibliothek, shelf mark C 4601.

title and the last word is eliminated? In reality, if we read the text of what became the final aphorism in the book, we find yet another bell: the morning bell.

This text, titled *The Wanderer* (*Der Wanderer*), ends with the image of travelers and philosophers who "ponder on how, between the tenth and the twelfth stroke of the bell, the day could present a face so pure, so light-filled, so cheerful and transfigured: —they seek the *philosophy of the morning*."[49] It would seem, therefore, that the reference in the work's title to Plato's human things is still present, yet more hidden, for it is accessible only through another echo effect, that between the morning bell and the evening bell: the morning bell of aphorism 638 hence refers to the evening bell of aphorism 628, which also contains Plato's words on human things, which in turn refer to the title of the work. With these interlocking echo effects, it would seem that Nietzsche wishes to cover his tracks and make the echo effect between the *Menschliches* of the title and that of the aphorism on the bells less detectable. This is not surprising, for our author practices and theorizes the idea of constructing symmetries in order to hide them afterward and so as not to follow them through to the end: "My style is a *dance*, a play of symmetries of all kinds, and at once a surpassing and a parody of these symmetries."[50] On the other hand, all while maintaining an intertextual reference to the image of the bells, the switching of these two aphorisms gives the end of the book a more affirmative nature, which refers back to the *trotzdem* of aphorism 628 and at the same time reinforces it with a solar image of morning. He announces, moreover, the image of intellectual vagrancy and the philosophy of the morning that will later find their expression in *The Wanderer and His Shadow* and in *Daybreak*, as well as the themes of meridian joy and the azure bell, which will be developed in *Thus Spoke Zarathustra*.

This final aphorism also contains a hidden homage to the Sorrentino gestation of the book. Indeed, we read in it: "if he relaxes quietly beneath the trees in the equanimity of his soul at morning, good and bright things will be thrown down to him from their tops and leaf hiding-places, the gifts of all those free spirits who are at home in mountain, wood, and solitude and who, like him, are, in their now joyful, now thoughtful way, wanderers and philosophers."[51] How can we read these lines without thinking of the tree in Sorrento from which, as Nietzsche related to Malwida, the thoughts of the philosophy of the free spirit fell onto his head (see above, chapter 4)? The image of Zarathustra's thoughts falling from trees like ripe figs returns in the chapter of *Thus Spoke Zarathustra* "Upon the Blessed Isles": "The figs are falling from the trees; they are good and sweet; and, as they fall, their red skin bursts. I am a north wind to ripe figs. Thus, like figs, these teachings fall to you, my friends; now consume their juice and their sweet meat. It is autumn about us, and pure sky and afternoon."[52] Furthermore, as we have seen, when he imagined the blessed isles, Nietzsche was thinking of the isle of Ischia, on which he had often gazed in Sorrento, from the terrace of the Villa Rubinacci.[53]

THE AZURE BELL OF INNOCENCE

The image of the azure bell is ancient too, and goes back to Nietzsche's first philosophical readings as an adolescent. In the pages of Ralph Waldo Emerson's *Conduct of Life*, Nietzsche had found the description of the glass bell of the celestial horizon:

> In childhood, we fancied ourselves walled in by the horizon, as by a glass bell, and doubted not, by distant travel, we should reach the baths of the descending sun and stars. On experiment, the horizon flies before us, and leaves us on an endless common, sheltered by no glass bell. Yet it is strange how tenaciously we cling to that bell-astronomy, of a protecting domestic horizon.[54]

The philosopher will use this Emersonian notion to explain his doctrine of innocence in becoming, comparing it to an azure bell that protects life from the erroneous and harmful interpretations of metaphysics and teleology. The celestial bell of immanence reassures us and returns to us the serenity of the one who knows that nothing exists outside of our earthly world: no god, no metaphysical dimension, no Schopenhauerian will to live; and that becoming is not the manifestation of Christian providence, nor of Hegelian rationality, nor of a moral or biological tendency toward an ultimate end, as those who were considered to be the great philosophers of the time had proposed: Eduard von Hartmann, Eugen Dühring, and Herbert Spencer. The doctrine of innocence in becoming is equivalent to a blessing of the world, because if no metaphysical or teleological dimension exists, then existence regains all of its value. In the chapter "Before Sunrise" of *Thus Spoke Zarathustra*, the Persian wise man explains the effect of his doctrine of innocence:

> But this is my blessing: to stand over every single thing as its own heaven, as its own round roof, its azure bell, and eternal security; and blessed is he who blesses thus. [...]
>
> Verily, it is a blessing and not a blasphemy when I teach: "Over all things stand the heaven Accident, the heaven Innocence, the heaven Chance, the heaven Prankishness."
>
> "By Chance"—that is the most ancient nobility of the world, and this I restored to all things: I delivered them from their bondage under Purpose. This freedom and heavenly cheer I have placed over all things like an azure bell when I taught that over them and through them no "eternal will" wills.[55]

Even the feeling of bliss that this perfect world in itself provides, with no need to approach a goal or obey a moral principle, is expressed with images and words that come from Emerson. In his *Essays*, Emerson had described all-encompassing moments when the world reaches its perfection and man attains ecstasy: "There are days which occur in this climate, at almost any season of the year, wherein the world reaches its perfection, when the air, the heavenly bodies, and the earth, make a harmony, as if nature would indulge her offspring [...]. The day, immeasurably long, sleeps over the broad hills and warm wide fields." Nietzsche had been struck by this image and had used it in a letter to Gersdorff: "Dear friend, sometimes, there are hours of quiet contemplation when one regards his life with a mixture of joy and sorrow, like the beautiful summer days, which largely lie on hills at ease and which Emerson describes so admirably: then, as he says, nature reaches its perfection and we are freed from the spells of the ever-wakeful will, then we are nothing but pure, contemplating, disinterested eye." In this letter of his youth, Nietzsche interprets Emerson's image in Schopenhauerian terms, as a moment of peace of the will to live and of pure contemplation of the knowing subject.[56] The image returns in the chapter "At Noon," purified of the Schopenhauerian interpretation and pervaded with a classical feeling of meridian, all-encompassing astonishment, combined with the sensation of an instant of fleeting and intense happiness:

> Still! Still! Did not the world become perfect just now? What is happening to me? [. . .]
>
> O happiness! O happiness! Would you sing, O my soul? You are lying in the grass. But this is the secret solemn hour when no shepherd plays his pipe.
>
> Refrain! Hot noon sleeps on the meadows. Do not sing! Still! The world is perfect. Do not sing, you winged one in the grass, O my soul—do not even whisper! Behold—still!—the old noon sleeps, his mouth moves: is he not just now drinking a drop of happiness,
>
> an old brown drop of golden happiness, golden wine? It slips over him, his happiness laughs.[57]

ZARATHUSTRA'S NIGHT SONG

In two key chapters of the third and fourth parts of *Thus Spoke Zarathustra*, the image of the bell of nihilism that we discovered in the episode at Genoa returns. In the chapter "The Other Dancing Song," penultimate to the final part, the bell of nihilism appears in the form of an old tenor bell that rings out at midnight and, as in the Genoa notebook, this image is associated with the desire for death. Life speaks to Zarathustra thoughtfully and tells him, in a soft voice:

> "O Zarathustra, you are not faithful enough to me.
>
> You do not love me nearly as much as you say; I know you are thinking of leaving me soon.
>
> There is an old heavy, heavy growl-bell that growls at night all the way up to your cave;
>
> when you hear this bell strike the hour at midnight, then you think between one and twelve—
>
> you think, O Zarathustra, I know it, of how you want to leave me soon"

But this time, in the face of the bell of nihilism, Nietzsche does not settle for formulating a timid objection, for adding a *trotzdem*. He finally finds a response to Plato's words. He murmurs it first into the ear of life:

"Yes," I answered hesitantly, "but you also know—" and I whispered something into her ear, right through her tangled yellow foolish tresses.
"You *know* that, O Zarathustra? Nobody knows that."[58]

Then Zarathustra pronounces, or rather, sings his response to the rhythm of the twelve strokes of the bell of nihilism. No longer do Plato's words accompany the peal of the bells at dusk, but it is Zarathustra's round, born of a deeper pain and a deeper joy, that resounds in counterpoint to the old tenor bell of midnight:

One!
O man, take care!
Two!
What does the deep midnight declare?
Three!
"I was asleep, I was asleep—
Four!
"From a deep dream I awoke:
Five!
"The world is deep,
Six!
"Deeper than day had been aware.
Seven!
"Deep is its woe;
Eight!
"Joy—deeper still than agony:
Nine!
"Woe commands: Begone!
Ten!
"But all joy wants eternity—
Eleven!
"Wants deep, deep eternity."
Twelve![59]

Zarathustra is the master of the eternal return and thus the response to Plato is the doctrine of the eternal return of the same. And yet this is strange, because the eternal return is a doctrine that expresses the extreme form of nihilism, and it is the strongest traditional argument used by pessimistic philosophers to devalorize earthly existence and turn the human gaze toward the suprasensible, the eternal, the immovable. Let us think of the "nothing new under the sun" or the "all is vanity" of Ecclesiastes.[60] Or of Leopardi's almanac seller who would agree to relive the years he has lived on the condition of having a different life.[61] According to Schopenhauer: "perhaps at the end of his life, no man, if he be sincere and at the same time in possession of his faculties, will ever wish to go through it again. Rather than this, he will much prefer to choose complete nonexistence." And, condensing his pessimism into a single sentence, he added: "If we knocked on the graves and asked the dead whether they would like to rise again, they would shake their heads."[62] Eduard von Hartmann considered the repetition of the identical to be the irrefutable demonstration of the pessimistic doctrine. In a central passage of his book, the chapter titled "The Unreasonable Nature of the Will and the Misery of Existence," he imagines that death asks a satisfied and opulent member of the bourgeoisie if he would agree to relive his existence:

> Let's imagine a man who is not a genius, who hasn't received any more than the general education of any modern man; who possesses all advantages of an enviable position, and finds himself in the prime of life. A man with a full awareness of the advantages he enjoys, when compared to the lower members of society, to the savage nations, and to the men of the Barbarian ages; a man who does not envy those above him, and who knows that their lives are plagued with inconveniences that he is spared; a man, finally, who is not exhausted, not blasé with joy, and not repressed by any exceptional personal misfortunes. Let us suppose that death comes and finds this man and addresses him in these terms: "The span of your life has expired, the time has come when you must become the prey of nothingness. Yet, it is up to you to choose if you wish to start again—in the same conditions, with full forgetting of the past—your life that is now over. Now choose!"
>
> I doubt that our man would prefer to start again the preceding life-play rather than enter nothingness.[63]

In his own turn, Nietzsche had reused this image in the first public formulation of the doctrine of the eternal return, the famous aphorism 341 of *The Gay Science*. This time, it is a demon who, stealing into man's loneliest loneliness, asks him if he wants to relive life as he has lived it. According to *The Gay Science*, there are two possible ways of responding to such a question. The normal response is a desperate refusal: "Would you not throw yourself down and gnash your teeth and curse the demon who spoke thus?" But Nietzsche also introduces the possibility of accepting the return: "Or have you once experienced a tremendous moment when you would have answered him: 'You are a god and never have I heard anything more divine.'"[64] *The Gay Science* tells us precisely this: that Nietzsche foresaw the possibility of an affirmative response to the demon's question. In "The Other Dancing Song" of *Thus Spoke Zarathustra*, Nietzsche makes fun by parodying Schopenhauer, Hartmann, and himself; for this time it is neither life nor death nor a demon who speaks of the eternal return as a terrible threat to man who lives agreeably, but it is Zarathustra who, desperate and close to suicide, announces the doctrine of the eternal return to life. But what exactly did Zarathustra murmur into life's ear, "through her tangled yellow foolish tresses"? He certainly didn't accost her with an essay on the laws of thermodynamics and on cosmological antinomies, on the arguments demonstrating the philosophical and scientific plausibility of the hypothesis of the eternal return. Moreover, these arguments were well known by the culture of the time: the eternal return was one of the theories that enriched the scientific debate. For example, Ludwig Boltzmann, independently of Nietzsche, would present the theory at the end of his famous lessons on the kinetic theory of gases.[65] But this is not what Zarathustra discovered. Zarathustra murmurs to life the new meaning that the eternal return has for him. He confides in life that he has lived a prodigious instant and that, for love of this instant, all human things have now gained a prodigious value for him, because all other events are collectively bound to this very instant and will necessarily return with it.

This interpretation is confirmed in the penultimate chapter of the fourth part of *Zarathustra*, "The Sleepwalker's Song"—the twin of "The Other Dancing Song," which is the penultimate chapter of the third part—in which we hear the new midnight bell. After the festival of the ass, a certain thing happens "which, on that whole long amazing day, was the most amazing thing of all": the ugliest man, one of the higher men to which the fourth part of *Zarathustra* is dedicated, reveals that he has learned to love life and to will the eternal return. For the principal goal of *Thus Spoke Zarathustra* is to announce the thought of the eternal return, but this announcement is made in several steps arranged according to a precise rhetorical progression. The narrative style allows Nietzsche to simultaneously stage Zarathustra's process of maturation in assimilating the eternal return and the effects that this doctrine produces on different human types. This progression by no means indicates a change in the doctrine's contents,[66] but expresses a change in the protagonist and his interlocutors. The thought of the eternal return slowly matures Zarathustra, and his maturation takes place by his confrontation with different ways of perceiving circular temporality, which in turn correspond to different levels of the historical sense. The more developed the historical sense, the more difficult it is to accept the eternal return. Zarathustra's animals, for example, have no fear of the eternal return for the simple reason that they have no historical memory. The ugliest man, on the other hand, is the very personification of the historical sense: he knows all the pain and all the absurdity of human history, and is aware of how difficult it is to bear the repetition of this succession of massacres and disappointed hopes.[67] And yet, after meeting Zarathustra, the ugliest man declares:

> "For the sake of this day, *I* am for the first time satisfied that I have lived my whole life.
>
> "And that I attest so much is still not enough for me. Living on earth is worthwhile: one day, one festival with Zarathustra, taught me to love the earth.
>
> "'Was *that* life?' I want to say to death. 'Well then! Once more!'"

At this very moment, the old tenor bell starts to chime out midnight, reciting the commented verses of its round. In this case too, as in the dialogue with life, it is pointless for Zarathustra to present the contents of his doctrine in detail in his commentary. Higher men know it. *Thus Spoke Zarathustra* sought, rather, to create a philosophical context in which the eternal return could be accepted not only by animals, but also by the most refined intellects of the era. After the words of the ugliest man had been spoken, the higher men "all at once became conscious of how they had changed and convalesced and to whom they owed this."[68]

In his commentary on the song of the bell, Zarathustra attempts to explain how the strongest symbol of nihilism can be transformed into an affirmation of existence. "The Sleepwalker's Song" is composed of twelve paragraphs. In the sixth, which functions as a key to the vault, the words and images begin, almost imperceptibly, to be colored by sweetness and bliss. Nietzsche writes: "Sweet lyre! Sweet lyre! I love your sound, your drunken toad's croaking. From how long ago, from how far away your sound comes to me, from the distant ponds of love!"[69] The reader of *Zarathustra* notices two surprising variations: the lyre of despairing repetition has grown sweet, and the toad, which embodied the bad omen, has become drunk and now sings from the ponds of love. Let us see why. The term *Leier* means lyre but also hurdy-gurdy (*Drehleier*), an ancient instrument in which the strings are set into vibration by a wheel that a handle works and that turns constantly. In popular language, *Es its immer die gleiche Leier* means "it is always the same tune." This expression lends itself very well to expressing the nihilistic version of the eternal return, the nothing new under the sun. Schopenhauer, moreover, used the term *Leierstück* in paragraph 58 of *World as Will and Representation*, just before inquiring whether the dead would want to relive their life:

> It is really incredible how meaningless and insignificant when seen from without, and how dull and senseless when felt from within, is the course of life of the great majority of men. [. . .] They [men] are like clockwork that is wound up and goes without knowing why. Every time a man is begotten and born, the clock of human life is wound up anew, to repeat once more its same old tune [*Leierstück*] that has already been played innumerable times, movement by movement and measure by measure, with insignificant variations.[70]

Besides the use of the word in "The Sleepwalker's Song," *Leier* is used in only one other parable of *Zarathustra*: "The Convalescent." In this parable, the animals present the doctrine of the eternal return and Zarathustra calls them *Drehorgeln*, barrel organs, and reproaches them for having made of his doctrine a *Leier-Lied*, a hurdy-gurdy song. The animals then advise Zarathustra to make himself a new lyre (*Leier*), more compatible with the songs (*Lieder*) that he must sing: no longer the old song of nothing new under the sun, but the song of the joyous acceptance of the return. And it is precisely accompanied by this new "sweet lyre" that Zarathustra sings over the strokes of the midnight tenor bell. Also, the term *Unke*, meaning literally "yellow-bellied toad" or generally, "fire-bellied toad," is used only in two parables of *Zarathustra*. The fire-bellied toad is a small amphibian similar to a generic toad that lives in ponds, but in German, in a figurative sense, the verb *unken* means to be pessimistic, to seek out bad omens. In the parable, "On Priests," Zarathustra had said: "As corpses they meant to live; in black they decked out their corpses; out of their speech, too, I still smell the bad odor of death chambers. And whoever lives near them lives near black ponds in which an ominous toad sings its song with sweet melancholy."[71] Yet now, after even the ugliest man has accepted the return, the sound of the lyre of the bad omen grows sweet and Zarathustra henceforth loves its drunken toad song (*trunkenen Unken-Ton*), which no longer comes from black ponds but from the ponds of love.

The old tenor bell of midnight too is transformed in this sixth paragraph of "The Sleepwalker's Song": "You old bell, you sweet lyre! Every pain has torn into your heart, father-pain, fathers' pain, forefathers' pain [*Vaterschmerz, Väterschmerz, Urväterschmerz*]; your speech grew ripe—"[72] Once more the biographical dimension surfaces, as the bell is once more associated with the death of his father, although the connection gains a larger meaning, of historical value. But the word, which has ripened through pain, no longer wants to die of despair but of happiness (*vor Glück sterben*), because while the old bell (*von altem Glocke*) rings out pain, a mysterious fragrance spreads toward the heights, like a scent of eternity rising from old happiness (*von altem Glücke*). Yet again there is the suggestion that a happiness from long ago, an instant of deep bliss, could release all pain and that pain and joy, *Glocke* and *Glücke*, are intimately related. The paragraph ends with the "drunken happiness of dying at midnight" (*trunkenem Mitternachts-Sterbeglücke*), which sings: the world is deep, deeper than day had been aware! To mark this passing, Nietzsche creates the word *Sterbeglücke*, happiness of death, a transformation of *Sterbeglocke*, the death knell.[73] The bell of pain now expresses a bliss that is stronger than death, while the madman's hurdy-gurdy becomes the sweetness of repetition, the sweet lyre of Zarathustra's round.

The draft of the ninth paragraph shows us how present the memory of the Genoa epiphany still is in "The Sleepwalker's Song."[74] Indeed, to annotate the line of the round: "Woe commands: Begone!" Nietzsche had written that woe longs for death (*sehnsüchtig nach dem Tode*), recovering the title of the Genoa aphorism on suicide titled *Sehnsucht nach dem Tode*, desire for death, of which we spoke earlier.

Finally, in the tenth paragraph of "The Sleepwalker's Song," the ugliest man's reasoning is formulated more explicitly. This explanation assumes and transforms the Faustian meaning of the instant. Goethe had written:

> If I say to the instant:
> Linger still! You are beautiful!
> Then you may shackle me in chains,
> Then I will happily die,
> Then the death knell may resound.[75]

We will note that in Goethe's lines, a *Totenglocke*, a death knell, was already to be found. Zarathustra responds thus to Faust in his commentary on the tenth stroke of the bell of nihilism:

> Have you ever said Yes to a single joy? O my friends, then you have said Yes to *all* woe. All things are entangled, ensnared, enamored;

if you ever wanted one thing twice, if you ever said, "You please me, happiness!
   Abide, moment!" then you wanted *all* back.
All anew, all eternally, all entangled, ensnared, enamored—oh, then you *loved*
   the world. Eternal ones, love it eternally and evermore; and to woe too, you
   say: go, but return!
For all joy wants—eternity.[76]

The eternal return is the most radical response possible to philosophical
or scientific teleologies, as well as to the linear temporality of the Christian
tradition: in the cosmos of the eternal return, there is no longer any place
for creation, providence, or redemption. It is no longer possible to stop or
to direct time: every instant flees but is destined to return, identical—for our
greatest happiness or greatest misfortune. But then, *who* would have desired to
relive the same existence anew? Who could rejoice in pulling the arrow from
the hand of the god Chronos to put the ring onto the finger of eternity? Goethe
sought an instant to which he could say: "linger still, you are beautiful." Nietzsche, for his part, waits for a man who could say to *every* instant: "pass and
return, identical, for all eternity."

Here, two images merge: the black tenor bell of midnight and the azure bell
of noon. And indeed, in the tenth paragraph of "The Sleepwalker's Song,"
slightly before the words that we have quoted, we read: "Just now my world
became perfect; midnight too is noon."[77] The eternal return thus unites the
perfect world, filled with the happiness of noon and its reassuring bell of immanence with the nihilism of midnight: if you have said Yes to a single instant
of pleasure, then you have also assented to the midnight bell and to all of the
woe that it carries with it. Day is stronger than night, affirmation than negation,
pleasure than pain.[78] It is for this reason that the phrase "the world is deep,
deeper than day had been aware" is first uttered when Zarathustra speaks of
the azure bell, in the chapter "Before Sunrise" and is later repeated in the
round of the midnight tenor bell.[79]

EPILOGUE TO THE BELL

Our story is not over: there is an epilogue, an epilogue to the song of the bell.
In 1885, Nietzsche plans to rewrite *Things Human, All Too Human* in view of
an edition of his complete works. The project will not be completed, but his
notebooks retain the trace of this work. In one of his notes, the philosopher
returns to the main themes of the book and concludes with the following ex-
clamation:

IV Schluß: In Genua: Oh meine Freunde. Versteht ihr dieß "Trotzdem"? ——[80]

Nietzsche thus shows that he is perfectly aware of the fact that aphorism 628 is the true conclusion, *Schluß*, of the book, and that the meaning of this writing is contained precisely in the "and yet," in the challenge that the author takes up to the Platonic tradition in the wake of the Genoa epiphany. We have seen that in *The Birth of Tragedy*, human things had value only in relation to the metaphysics of art and that when Nietzsche no longer believes in metaphysics, he must say, with Plato, or better, with Leopardi, that no human thing is worthy of value. But afterward, the addition of a *trotzdem* opens a range of possibilities within a resigned yet active skepticism that is concerned with imminent things and that holds, with Epicurus, that some human things have value. Until the point when, thanks to the thought of the eternal return, all human things finally acquire a great value.

CHAPTER SIX

Torna a Surriento

In remembrance of his first stay in Sorrento, Nietzsche will often dream of following the advice of the Italian song *Torna a Surriento*, "Return to Sorrento." Already in September 1877, during a night of insomnia spent delighting in beautiful images of Sorrentino nature, he considers the possibility of living in the heights of the isle of Capri, in Anacapri.[1] In the summer of 1879, Nietzsche again considers spending the winter in the countryside surrounding Naples. But word reaches him that Wagner is planning to move there—which he will do beginning in January 1880. Nietzsche thus prefers to abandon his plans.

> *No one* will know anything about my winter plans except you. I would love the countryside near Naples most of all (a great many sunny days, the essential thing! and many walks: the latter are lacking in Venice, and solitude pushes me forward much more than the company of Köselitz or Rée, I see that now—I must simply have a *great variety* of walks to choose from, as I have here[2]), but against Naples, there is Wagner's presence.[3]

Instead, he is persuaded to travel north, where he will spend "the most sunless winter of my entire life," the winter during which, seriously ill, he looks death in the face for the first time. In the autumn of 1880, he makes another attempt to renew his ties with the South: Nietzsche travels to Genoa to take the boat for Castellammare di Stabia, near Naples, but he changes his mind at the last minute and decides to remain in Genoa. He will never again return to the Gulf of Naples.

Perhaps he sensed that he wouldn't be able to stand the view of these places with which so many memories were associated: Wagner's confessions about the Eucharist, the image of young Brenner, who had since died of tuberculosis, the friendship with Paul Rée, broken after the Lou von Salomé affair. Only Malwida remained for him, the dear idealistic friend who was still waiting for Nietzsche to return to the metaphysics of the artist in *The Birth of Tragedy* and who, in the meantime, between the maestro of Bayreuth and the philosopher of the free spirit, wandering and solitary, remained faithful . . . to Wagner. The philosopher and the old countess knew that another journey together was no longer possible, but they both retained a tender memory of this period of happiness in Sorrento.

In 1887, ten years after this unique stay, after having unwound the whole line of thoughts that had been awakened on the slopes of Vesuvius, after accomplishing the parable of the free spirit and drawing from it the final consequences, Nietzsche remembers once more, with pleasure and with a particular nostalgia, the liberation he had experienced in the midst of the community at the Villa Rubinacci, where, for the first time, he had exercised his lungs and his intellect in the fresh and invigorating air of the philosophy of the free spirit.

Yet another winter in your company, with you and perhaps even with the cultivation and care of Trina—that is indeed the highest and most alluring prospect and perspective, for which I could never thank you enough! Preferably once again in Sorrento (δὶς καὶ τρὶς τὸ καλὸν, the Greeks say, "all that is good needs a second time, a third time!"). Or in Capri—where I will play music for you again, but better than before! Or in Amalfi or Castellammare. Perhaps finally even in Rome (although my mistrust of the Roman climate, and of large cities in general, is grounded on good reasons and is not easy to overturn). Solitude with the most solitary nature has always been my relief, my means of recovery: in the end, cities of modern commotion like Nice, and even like Zurich (where I just came from) make me irritable, gloomy, unsure, despondent, unproductive, ill. I have retained a kind of yearning and superstition from our stay *down there*, as though, if only for a couple of moments, I had breathed more deeply there than anywhere else. For example, on our very first drive through Naples, as we made our way together to Posillipo. ——[4]

When, during the summer of 1900, death freed the philosopher, long insane and infirm, from his suffering, Malwida was precisely down there. She sent a branch of laurels to Weimar from Sorrento, as a last farewell from the land of sirens.[5]

Twenty-three years after this winter that I had lived with him in Sorrento, I found myself once again spending the summer in this lovely place. The memory of that time came back to me so vividly that the Nietzsche of the old days seemed completely alive to me. I saw him again, laughing joyously as he walked along the narrow paths bordered by walls, above which the high orange trees moved their branches about, covered in golden fruit [. . .]. I heard him, sitting cozily in the evening in our little circle, give the most beautiful commentaries on Jacob Burckhardt's courses on Greek culture and heard his gay laughter at the whimsical ideas of our young companion Brenner or at the stories of comical events that had taken place in the once primitive conditions of the little village (it has since been considerably modernized). The memory attained such clarity that I felt the need to trace out the form of my friend from the first time of our meeting to the end. Then, on August 26, along with the newspaper, a telegram of the twenty-fifth came from Weimar and something cried out in me: praise God, the nightmare is over at last! This is why the image of the Nietzsche of long ago was so vividly present in my mind the whole time; the hard battle has been fought: the heroic sufferer, the weary fighter can now rest, and the young Nietzsche lives for all time, smiling gently, in his original harmony, with the concluding words of all true philosophy on his lips: "All that is perishable is only a symbol."[6]

Keeping resolutely to the young Nietzsche, the Nietzsche of *The Birth of Tragedy*, Malwida seeks to exorcize not only the ten years of madness but the whole philosophy of the free spirit, Nietzsche's true philosophy, which she had never accepted. Of course, the poets and the metaphysicians, from Parmenides to Goethe, have often imagined that this "passing" world is only a symbol of something that endures eternally, but Malwida knew perfectly well that the poet-prophet Zarathustra, the living parody of all the poets and of all the prophets, had expressed himself quite differently when, speaking "upon the blessed isles"—that is, upon the isle of Ischia—he had taught that all that is *im*perishable is only a symbol and that poets lie too much:

Evil I call it, and misanthropic: all this teaching of the One and the Plenum and the Unmoved and the Sated and the Imperishable!
All that is imperishable—that is only a symbol! And the poets lie too much.
It is of time and becoming that the best symbols should speak: let them be a praise and a justification of all that is perishable![7]

Nietzsche would have preferred the fool's cap to the poet's laurels, for if the poet lies, the fool speaks, or rather, *laughs* the truth, a truth that tells of the body and becoming. But that was doubtless too difficult to explain to the good idealist Malwida or even to Elisabeth, Nietzsche's sister, the Teuton and bigot who, after the pretty Christian funeral, prepared to bury the philosopher of the free spirit at the foot of the little church in Röcken, where he was born. Why not instead in Sorrento, where Nietzsche had experienced a new birth? Or on the blessed isle of Ischia.

NOTES

1. Cf. *The Birth of Tragedy*, § 4 and 5 (eKGWB/GT-4 and 5) and the ulterior self-criticism that he formulates in *Thus Spoke Zarathustra*, I, "On the Afterworldly," eKGWB/Za-I-Hinterweltler.

2. Friedrich Nietzsche, *The Birth of Tragedy*, § 23, eKGWB/GT-23. *The Birth of Tragedy*, trans. Walter Kaufmann (New York: Random House, 1967), 135. Trans. mod.

3. Cf. Sandro Barbera, *Guarigioni, rinascite e metamorfosi. Studi su Goethe, Schopenhauer e Nietzsche* (Firenze: Le lettere, 2010), 135ff.

4. Cf. posthumous fragment eKGWB/NF-1879,40[11].

5. Posthumous fragment eKGWB/NF-1879,40[9]. My trans. Again in 1885, when Nietzsche thought back to *The Birth of Tragedy*, he spoke of "a desire for tragic myth (for 'religion' and, indeed, for a pessimistic religion) (as a protective bell where growing things thrive)," eKGWB/NF-1885,2[110]. My trans.

6. *Ecce Homo*, chap. titled "Things Human, All Too Human," § 4, eKGWB/EH-MA-4. My trans.

7. Posthumous fragment eKGWB/NF-1876,23[159]. My trans.

8. On the importance of the Sorrento period for the periodization of Nietzsche's philosophy, I have already expressed myself in "Système, phases diachroniques, strates synchroniques, chemins thématiques," in Paolo D'Iorio and Olivier Ponton, eds., *Nietzsche. Philosophie de l'esprit libre* (Paris: Éditions Rue d'Ulm, 2004), 24ff. The philosophical and linguistic reasons for which I translate *Menschliches, Allzumenschliches* as *Things Human, All Too Human* (*Choses humaines, bien trop humaines*), instead of the standard *Human, All Too Human*, are explained in chap. 5, in "Crossed Geneses."

9. Posthumous fragment eKGWB/NF-1875,5[190]. My trans. This thought is generalized in aphorism 619 of *Things Human, All Too Human*, eKGWB/MA-619.

10. *Ecce Homo*, chap. titled "Things Human, All Too Human," § 3, eKGWB/EH-MA-3. *On the Genealogy of Morals* and *Ecce Homo*, trans. Walter Kaufmann (New York: Random House, 1989), *Ecce Homo*, "*Things Human, All Too Human*," § 3, 286–87. Trans. mod.

11. Posthumous fragment eKGWB/NF-1876, 19 [68], facsimile DFGA/U-II-5,57; Spinoza, *Ethica*, IV, 67.

CHAPTER ONE

1. Charles Andler, *Nietzsche, sa vie et sa pensée* (Paris: Gallimard, 1958), vol. II, 273.

2. Cf. Nietzsche to his sister, July 28, 1875, from Bayreuth: "My journey to Italy is arranging itself even more beautifully than I could have wished. Sea and forest and close to Naples—it is there that we might go. Let us only hope," eKGWB/BVN-1876,545. My trans.

3. Malwida von Meysenbug, *Der Lebensabend einer Idealistin* (Berlin: Schuster & Loeffler, 1898), 44–46; cf. Nietzsche to Malwida, May 11, 1876, eKGWB/BVN-1876,523. My trans.

4. As Renate Müller-Buck explains, "'Immer wieder kommt einer zur Gemeine hinzu.' Nietzsches junger Basler Freund und Schüler Albert Brenner," in *Centauren-Geburten. Wissenschaft, Kunst und Philosophie beim jungen Nietzsche*, ed. T. Brosche, F. Gerratana, and A. Venturelli (Berlin-New York: Walter de Gruyter, 1994), 430.

5. On this matter, see legal expert Eduard His's study, in Eduard His and Hans Gutzwiller, *Friedrich Nietzsches Heimatlosigkeit. Friedrich Nietzsches Lehrtätigkeit am Basler Pädagogium 1869–1875* (Basel: Schwabe, 2002.)

6. Cf. the letters to Franz Overbeck of August 20–21, 1881, and December 6, 1881, eKGWB/BVN-1881, 139 and 176.

7. Nietzsche to his mother and sister, October 9, 1876, eKGWB/BVN-1876,558. My trans.

8. Rée to Nietzsche, October 10, 1877, KGB II/6/2, 717. My trans.

9. Nietzsche to Elisabeth, October 18, 1876, eKGWB/BVN-1876,562. My trans.

10. Nietzsche to Wagner, September 27, 1876, eKGWB/BVN-1876,556. My trans. In his autobiography, Wagner relates that after a difficult sea journey between Genoa and La Spezia in September of 1853, hoping to find rest in a hotel bed, he had been overcome by the sensation of color in the water and that this sensation was expressed in the harmony of E-flat major in rippling arpeggios. This gave him the germ of the beginning of *Rheingold* and thus of the entire cycle of *The Ring of the Nibelung*; cf. Richard Wagner, *Mein Leben* (München: List, 1963), 512.

11. Nietzsche to Elisabeth, October 22, 1876, eKGWB/BVN-1876,563. My trans.

12. "Yes, the work emerges more beautiful / From a material rebellious to work— / Verse, marble, onyx, enamel— / No false oppositions, / But to walk straight— / Muse, you don / A slender shoe." My trans.

13. "The bust will survive the city." From *Émaux et Camées (Enamels and Cameos)*. My trans.

14. Isabelle von Ungern-Sternberg, *Nietzsche im Spiegelbild seiner Schrift* (Leipzig: Naumann, 1902), 26–30. My trans.

15. See the posthumous fragments eKGWB/NF-1870,5[1], [22], [41], [42]. For the relationship between the artistic genius and the philosophical genius in the new culture of Bayreuth, I refer to the introduction to Friedrich Nietzsche, *Les philosophes préplatoniciens* (Combas: Éditions de l'éclat, 1994), 11–49.

16. See Vivetta Vivarelli, *Nietzsche und die Masken des freien Geistes. Montaigne, Pascal und Sterne* (Würzburg: Königshausen & Neumann, 1998); cf. also David Molner, "The Influence of Montaigne on Nietzsche: A Raison d'Être in the Sun," *Nietzsche-Studien* 21 (1993), 80–93.

Nietzsche owned a beautiful copy of Montaigne's *Essais,* which Cosima and Richard Wagner had given him for Christmas in 1870 and which is still preserved today at the Herzogin Anna Amalia Bibliotek in Weimar (shelf mark C 300): Michel de Montaigne, *Versuche* (Leipzig: Lankischens Erben, 1753), 3 vols.; cf. the letter to Franziska and Elizabeth Nietzsche of December 30, 1870, eKGWB/BVN-1870,116.

17. Posthumous fragments eKGWB/NF-1876,16[8] and [28]. My trans.

18. Aphorism 283 of *Things Human, All Too Human,* eKGWB/MA-283, the drafts of which are contained in notebook N II 1, 48, DFGA/N-II-1,48. English edition: Friedrich Nietzsche, *Human All Too Human,* trans. R. J. Hollingdale (Cambridge: Cambridge University Press, 1996), 132.

19. Posthumous fragment eKGWB/NF-1876,16[7]. My trans.

20. Posthumous fragments eKGWB/NF-1876, 17 [74] and [85]. My trans. Cf. posthumous fragments eKGWB/NF-1876,16[8] and [9]. On this theme, see the innovative study by Olivier Ponton, *Philosophie de la légèreté* (Berlin/New York: de Gruyter, 2007).

21. Posthumous fragments eKGWB/NF-1876, 16[33], [34]. My trans.

22. *Things Human, All Too Human,* aphorism 225, eKGWB/MA-225. Trans. Hollingdale in *Human, All Too Human,* 108. Trans. mod.

23. *Things Human, All Too Human,* aphorism 230, eKGWB/MA-230. Trans. Hollingdale in *Human, All Too Human,* 110. Trans. mod.

24. Isabelle von Ungern-Sternberg, 28–29. My trans.

25. Nietzsche to Claudine von Brevern, October 23, 1876, eKGWB/BVN-1876,564. My trans.

26. Isabelle von Ungern-Sternberg, 30–31. My trans. Achates is a Trojan, the faithful friend of Aeneas, whom he accompanied on his travels, through to Italy (Virgil, *Aeneid,* 1, 120).

27. *The Wanderer and His Shadow,* Dialogue, eKGWB/WS-[Dialog]. Trans. Hollingdale in *Human, All Too Human,* 301. Trans. mod.

28. Cf. Georges Santi, "Mémoire sur les chameaux de Pise," in *Annales du Museum d'histoire naturelle,* no. 18, Paris, 1811, 320–30; Igino Cocchi, "Sur la naturalisation du dromadaire en Toscane," in *Bulletin mensuel de la société impériale zoologique d'acclimatation* (Paris: Masson, 1858), 473–82; Giovanni R. Fascetti, *I cammelli di San Rossore* (Pisa: Giardini, 1991). Cf. Stefano Busellato and Giuliano Campioni, *Tra la Torre e i cammelli. Nietzsche a Pisa* (Pisa: ETS, 2013).

29. Brenner to his family, October 26, 1876. My trans. Thirteen letters of Brenner's from Sorrento are conserved in the archives of the State of Basel and have been partially published in Carl Albrecht Bernoulli, *Franz Overbeck und Friedrich Nietzsche, eine Freundschaft* (Jena: Diederichs, 1908), vol. I, 198–207, and in Ruth Stummann-Bowert, ed., *Malwida von Meysenbug, Paul Rée. Briefe an einen Freund* (Würzburg: Königshausen & Neumann, 1998), 207–14; cf. Renate Müller-Buch, 425–27.

30. Meysenbug to Olga Monod-Herzen, Saturday, October 28, 1876, in Malwida von Meysenbug, *Im Anfang war die Liebe. Briefe an ihre Pflegtocher,* ed. Berta Schleicher, 2nd ed. (München: Beck, 1926), 93. My trans.

31. Meysenbug, *Der Lebensabend einer Idealistin,* 46–47. My trans.

32. Posillipo, in Greek παυσίλυπον, means, precisely, the breaking of sorrows.

33. Posthumous fragments eKGWB/NF-1881,12[142]; [177]; [181]; facsimiles DFGA/N-V-7, 120, 80, 78. My trans. The quotation in the first fragment is taken, in a modified and parodic,

inverted sense, from Wagner's *Tristan and Isolde* (Act II, scene II), where the two lovers, consecrated by night, protest against the deceptions of day. Nietzsche had previously quoted this expression, in its original sense, in *Richard Wagner in Bayreuth*, § 4 (eKGWB/WB-4). The expression returns again, in the inverted sense, in "The Song of Melancholy" of *Thus Spoke Zarathustra*, see below.

CHAPTER TWO

1. Cf. Benito Iezzi, *Viaggiatori stranieri a Sorrento* (Sorrento: Di Mauro, 1989).

2. Malwida had, indeed, already come to Sorrento on October 24, as Cosima Wagner noted in her journal: "Visit from Malwida, who is looking for an apartment for friend Nietzsche and inspects several houses. She returns to Naples in the evening." *Cosima Wagner's Diaries, Volume One: 1869–1877*, ed. Martin Gregor-Dellin and Dietrich Mack, trans. Geoffrey Skelton (New York, London: Harcourt Brace Jovanovich, 1978), 929. German edition: Cosima Wagner, *Tagebücher*, Martin Gregor-Dellin and Dietrich Mack, eds. (München: Piper, 1976–1977).

3. Meysenbug to Olga Monod-Herzen, Saturday, October 28, 1876, in Meysenbug, *Im Anfang war die Liebe*, 93–94. My trans.

4. Brenner to his family, Wednesday, November 1, 1876, in Stummann-Bowert, 209. My trans.

5. In French in the text: "near Naples."

6. Nietzsche to Elisabeth, October 28, 1876, eKGWB/BVN-1876,565. My trans.

7. Cosima Wagner's Diaries, vol. 1, 921–22.

8. *Ibid.*, 925, 926, 927, 930.

9. *Ibid.*, 928.

10. *Ibid.*, 932.

11. See Mazzino Montinari, "Nietzsche e Wagner cent'anni fa" in *Su Nietzsche* (Roma: Editori Riuniti, 1981), 14–29, republished with modifications in *Nietzsche lesen* (Berlin: de Gruyter, 1982), 38–55 (English trans. Mazzino Montinari, *Reading Nietzsche*, trans. Greg Whitlock (Chicago: University of Illinois Press, 2003); see also the critical apparatus to *Richard Wagner in Bayreuth*, in KGW IV/4, 119–60.

12. Cosima Wagner's Diaries, vol. 1, 930.

13. *Ibid.*

14. Nietzsche to Meysenbug, February 21, 1883, eKGWB/BVN-1883,382. My trans. This letter was recovered at the end of the 1970s, among the papers of Romain Rolland and published for the first time in the Colli/Montinari edition. It allows for the rectification of the interpretation of the "mortal offense" put forth by the biographers (Curt von Westernhagen, Martin Gregor-Dellin, Curt Paul Janz). According to these interpreters, Nietzsche was referring to a series of malicious pieces of gossip on the origin of his illness as coming apparently from onanism or from the pederasty that circulated in 1882, during the second festival of Bayreuth and which were born from an exchange of letters between Wagner and Dr. Eiser, the doctor who treated Nietzsche and a fervent Wagnerian. These insinuations wounded Nietzsche (cf. the letter to Köstelitz of April 21, 1883, eKGWB/BVN-1883,403), but they were certainly not

the reason for their break, also because they appeared later. It is not to them that Nietzsche referred with the expression "mortal offense." As Montinari summarizes: "Beyond any human or personal affair, the central crux of the conflict between Nietzsche and Wagner was contained properly speaking in this insurmountable disagreement concerning Christianity" (*Su Nietzsche*, 26–29; cf. also the critical apparatus to the Italian edition of the correspondence (Milano: Adelphi, 2004), vol. IV, 754), while the critical apparatus to the German edition (KGB III/1, 348) provides no information.

15. Posthumous fragment eKGWB/NF-1885,34[205]. My trans.

16. Cf. *Things Human, All Too Human*, vol. II, preface, § 3, eKGWB/MA-II-Vorrede-3 and the drafts eKGWB/NF-1885,35[49] and 34[205]. See, in addition, the following passage, contained in KGW IV/4, 254: "he began speaking of the 'blood of the Redeemer,' there was even an hour when he confessed to me all the raptures that he knew how to draw from the Eucharist," as well as the posthumous fragment eKGWB/NF-1885,2[101]: "In a single glance, I realized that Wagner had indeed attained his goal, but only in the manner that Napoleon had attained Moscow—with so many losses at every step, irreparable losses, that just at the end of the whole deployment and seemingly at the moment of victory, destiny had already been decided. [. . .] Wagner speaking of the ecstasy he got from the Christian Eucharist: this was decisive for me, I considered him *conquered*." My trans.

17. Cosima Wagner's Diaries, vol. 1, 1144.

18. Meysenbug, *Der Lebensabend einer Idealistin*, 48–49. My trans.

19. Posthumous fragment eKGWB/NF-1885,41[2] § 3. My trans.

20. Posthumous fragment eKGWB/NF-1875,5[190], see Introduction, above.

21. *Ecce homo*, chap. titled "Things Human, All Too Human," § 5, eKGWB/EH-MA-5. Trans. Kaufmann in *On the Genealogy of Morals* and *Ecce Homo*, 288. Trans. mod. The chronological reconstruction is not entirely accurate, for the philosopher's book did not arrive in Bayreuth until April 1878, four months after *Parsifal* was sent. Nietzsche, however, is probably alluding to the fact that he had finished the manuscript of *Things Human, All Too Human* and that on January 10, Köselitz had sent it to the editor.

22. Nietzsche to Seydlitz, January 4, 1878, eKGWB/BVN-1878,678. My trans.

23. Nietzsche to Köstelitz, August 20, 1880, eKGWB/BVN-1880,49. My trans.

24. Meysenbug, *Der Lebensabend einer Idealistin*, 47–48. My trans.

25. Paul Rée to Elizabeth Nietzsche, November 11, 1876. My trans. Paul Rée's letters to the Nietzsche family have been published in the critical apparatus of the fourth volume of the Beck edition of Nietzsche's correspondence (Friedrich Nietzsche, *Historisch-kritische Gesamtausgabe, Briefe*, ed. Wilhelm Hoppe (Munich: Beck, 1941), 455ff.) as well as by Ernst Pfeiffer, ed., *Friedrich Nietzsche, Paul Rée, Lou von Salomé: die Dokumente ihrer Begegnung* (Frankfurt am Main: Insel-Verlag, 1970). Trans. fr. *Friedrich Nietzsche, Paul Rée, Lou von Salomé. Correspondance* (Paris: PUF, 1979), 19ff.

26. For the localization of the Villa Rubinacci, see Nino Cuomo's article: "Scoperta la villa di Nietzsche," *Match-Point* IV/3, March 1990. The Hotel Eden is at 25, *via* Correale (the old *via* Bernardino Rota); it has been enlarged and has sixty rooms and a restaurant called "Villa Rubinacci." There is another Villa Rubinacci in Sorrento, but it is not the one in which Nietzsche lived, contrary to what David Farrel Krell and Donal L. Bates suggest in their book, *The Good*

European. Nietzsche's Work Sites in Word and Image (Chicago/London: University of Chicago Press, 1997), 97–98, 115, 233.

27. Nietzsche to Louise Ott, December 16, 1876, eKGWB/BVN-1876,577. My trans.

28. Malwida to Olga Monod-Herzen, November 20, 1876, in *Im Anfang war die Liebe*, 96.

29. Malwida to Olga Monod-Herzen, November 13, 1876, in *Briefe von und an Malwida von Meysenbug* (Berlin: Schuster & Loeffler, 1920), 112. My trans. Cf. also Nietzsche's letter to Overbeck of December 6, 1876: "We have read a great deal of Voltaire: now it is Mainländer's turn," eKGWB/BVN-1876,573. My trans.

30. In French in the text: without embarrassment or awkwardness.

31. Malwida to Olga Monod-Herzen, March 3, 1877, in *Briefe von und an Malwida von Meysenbug*, 130. My trans.

32. Meysenbug, *Der Lebensabend einer Idealistin*, 56–57. My trans.

33. Nietzsche to Marie Baumgartner, February 4, 1877, eKGWB/BVN-1877,594. My trans.

34. Meysenbug, *Der Lebensabend einer Idealistin*, 49. This characterization of the Greek people is also recalled in Malwida's letter to Rée of June 8–10, 1877, in Stummann-Bowert, 128.

35. "Die Religion und die Reflexion waren pessimistisch, das Temperament aber optimistisch; daher die enorme Productivität [. . .] Das Volk war voll von elastischen Federkräften, daher das lebendige optimistische Temperament, das stets zu neuen Thaten reizt. Die Lebensanschauung aber ist ganz pessimistisch." The influence of Burckhardt's lessons on the Nietzschean conception of Hellenism in the period 1875–1878 first attracted Montinari's attention in the critical apparatus of the texts of these years (cf. KGW IV/4, *passim*). This thematic has been taken up and developed by Ponton, *Philosophie de la légèreté*, 8–19, 186–87, 221–23 and *passim*.

36. Cf. Montinari, *Su Nietzsche*, 103. For Gramsci's expression, see for example the letter to his brother Carlo of December 19, 1929, in Antonio Gramsci, *Lettere dal carcere* (Torrino: Einaudi, 1947), 115.

37. Posthumous fragments eKGWB/NF-1875,5[25] and eKGWB/NF-1875,4[5] and the letter to Seydlitz of September 24, 1876, eKGWB/BVN-1876,554. My trans. On the plan of a monastery for free spirits, see Hubert Treiber, "Wahlverwandtschaften zwischen Nietzsches Idee eines 'Klosters für freiere Geister' und Webers Idealtypus der puritanischen Sekte," *Nietzsche-Studien*, 21 (1992), 326–62.

38. Posthumous fragment eKGWB/NF-1876,23[136]. My trans.

39. Posthumous fragment eKGWB/NF-1876,17[50]. My trans.

40. Meysenbug, *Der Lebensabend einer Idealistin*, 57–58. Cf. Meysenbug, *Memoiren einer Idealistin* (Stuttgart: Auerbach, 1876).

41. Sander Gilman, ed., *Conversations with Nietzsche: A Life in the Words of His Contemporaries*, trans. David J. Parent (Oxford: Oxford University Press, 1987), 92. Trans. mod. For the German, see Reinhart von Seydlitz, "Friedrich Nietzsche: Briefe und Gespräche," in Sander Gilman, ed., *Begegnungen mit Nietzsche* (Bonn: Bouvier, 1981).

42. Nietzsche to Elisabeth, January 20, 1877, eKGWB/BVN-1877,589. My trans.

43. See, respectively, eKGWB/BVN-1876,573; 575; 576; 582; 584. My trans. Cf. Paul Rée, *Der Ursprung der moralischen Empfindung* (Chemnitz: Schmeitzner, 1877); English trans. Paul Rée, *The Origin of the Moral Sensations*, ed. and trans. Robin Small (Chicago: University of Illinois

Press, 2003). Concerning Brenner's novellas, see Müller-Buck, 427–28; one of these novellas was published in July 1877 under the title "Das flammende Herz," *Deutsche Rundschau*, 3/10 (1877), 1–11; Meysenbug, *Phädra: ein Roman* (Leipzig: Reissner, 1885), 3 vols.

44. Nietzsche to Cosima Wagner, December 19, 1876, eKGWB/BVN-1876,581. My trans. The first commentary on this letter was given by Montinari, *Nietzsche Lesen*, 38–43 (English trans. *Reading Nietzsche*, 36–37).

45. Posthumous fragment eKGWB/NF-1878,28[33]. My trans.

46. Nietzsche to Overbeck, eKGWB/BVN-1877,654. My trans.

47. Nietzsche to Rohde, eKGWB/BVN-1877,656. My trans.

48. Nietzsche to Elisabeth, eKGWB/BVN-1877,657. My trans.

49. *Assorted Opinions and Maxims,* eKGWB/VM-360. Trans. Hollingdale in *Human, All Too Human*, 293. Trans. mod.

50. "It seems presumptuous and even heinous to replace such an antiquity with a novelty and to oppose to such an accumulation of acts of piety and veneration the unities of becoming and the present" (*On the Utility and the Disadvantages of History for Life*, § 3, eKGWB/HL-3. My trans.).

51. Posthumous fragment 58[16] from 1867.

52. Posthumous fragment 57[51] from 1867ff. English trans. in *Writings from the Early Notebooks*, ed. Raymond Geuss, trans. Ladislaus Löb (Cambridge: Cambridge University Press, 2009), "On Schopenhauer," 1ff.

53. Posthumous fragment eKGWB/NF-1878,30[9]. My trans. In this fragment, Nietzsche alludes to the fourth book of *World as Will and Representation* devoted to the negation of the will to live. See also eKGWB/NF-1878,27[43]: "The living Schopenhauer has nothing to do with the metaphysicians. He is essentially a Voltairian, the fourth book is foreign to him." My trans.

54. Cf. Montinari, "Nietzsche contra Wagner: été 1878," in Marc Crépon, ed., *Nietzsche*, Cahiers de l'Herne (Paris: L'Herne, 2000), 237–44, and Paolo D'Iorio, "Système, phases diachroniques, strates synchroniques, chemins thématiques," in D'Iorio and Ponton, eds., *Nietzsche. Philosophie de l'esprit libre.*

55. Cosima Wagner to Nietzsche, January 1, 1877 (KGB II/6/I, 472–75). My trans.

56. Cosima Wagner's Diaries, vol. 1, 938.

57. Quoted in Richard Count du Moulin-Eckart, *Cosima Wagner*, trans. Catherine Alison Phillips (New York: Alfred A. Knopf, 1930), vol. II, 697–98.

58. *Thus Spoke Zarathustra*, "Tomb Song," eKGWB/Za-II-Grablied. Trans. Walter Kaufmann in *Thus Spoke Zarathustra* (New York: The Viking Press, 1954), 112–13. Trans. mod. On the meaning of "How did I endure it?," "Wie ertrug ich's nur?," which refers to Wagner's *Tristan*, see chap. 1, in "Naples: First Revelation of the South."

59. Cosima Wagner to Nietzsche, 473. My trans.

60. Ritschl to Nietzsche, February 14, 1872, KGB II/2, 541. My trans.

61. Ritschl to Nietzsche, January 14, 1876, KGB II/6/1, 274. My trans.

62. Nietzsche to Sophie Ritschl, January 1877, eKGWB/BVN-1877,585. My trans. Friedrich Ritschl died November 9; the death notice that Nietzsche received in Sorrento is conserved at Weimar, GSA, 71/BW175.

CHAPTER THREE

1. Nietzsche to Köselitz, November 14, 1876, eKGWB/BVN-1876,569. My trans.

2. Brenner to his family, December 19, 1876, in Stumman-Bovert, 211. My trans. "Falter fliegen im Sonnenstrahl" is a line from the poem "Das Tal des Espingo" by Paul Heyse.

3. Nietzsche to his family, January 8, 1877, eKGWB/BVN-1877,587. My trans.

4. Meysenbug to Olga Monod-Herzen, February 13, 1877, in *Briefe von und an Malwida von Meysenbug*, 122. My trans.

5. Posthumous fragment eKGWB/NF-1876,21[49]. My trans.

6. Posthumous fragment eKGWB/NF-1876,23[147]. My trans.

7. Meysenbug to Olga Monod-Herzen, February 16, 1877, in *Briefe von und an Malwida von Meysenbug*, 123–24. My trans.

8. In English in the text. —Trans.

9. Meysenbug to Olga Monod-Herzen, March 23, 1877, in *Briefe von und an Malwida von Meysenbug*, 133–34. My trans.

10. Meysenbug, *Stimmungsbilder* (Berlin und Leipzig: Schuster & Loeffler, 1905), 4th ed., 85–86. My trans.

11. Nietzsche to his mother, March 26, 1877, eKGWB/BVN-1877,601. My trans.

12. Posthumous fragments eKGWB/NF-1878,28[17], [22], [24], [34], [39]. My trans.

13. Ferdinand Gregorovius, *Figuren, Geschichte, Leben und Scenerie aus Italien* (Leipzig: Brockhaus, 1856), 360–62. My trans.

14. *Thus Spoke Zarathustra*, I, prologue, § 1, eKGWB/Za-I-Vorrede-1. Trans. Kaufmann, *Thus Spoke Zarathustra*, 10. Trans. mod.

15. Gregorovius, 362–63. My trans.

16. *Beyond Good and Evil*, aphorism 55, eKGWB/JGB-55. Trans. Kaufmann in *Beyond Good and Evil* (New York: Random House, 1966), 67.

CHAPTER FOUR

1. Reinhart von Seydlitz, in Gilman, 91–92.

2. *Ibid.*, 91. Trans. mod.

3. Posthumous fragment eKGWB/NF-1885,2[201]. My trans.

4. We have already had the occasion to quote notebook N II 1, which we have named the notebook of the free spirit. The Sorrento manuscripts also include two other notebooks classified in the Goethe-Schiller Archives at Weimar under the shelf marks N II 3 and N II 2, as well as two journals, U II 5 and M I 1, and a file of papers containing the final copy M XIV 1. See the description of the manuscripts of this period given by Montinari in KGW IV/4, 102–105.

5. Meysenbug, *Der Lebensabend einer Idealistin*, 66. My trans.

6. Meysenbug, *Individualitäten* (Berlin: Schuster & Loeffler, 1902), 26–27, 34. My trans. Nietzsche was well aware of Malwida's reason for not breaking with him, and he wrote to her in 1883: "For many years now I have been completely alone and you will admit that I have made 'a good face' to all of that—even the *good* face belongs among the conditions of my asceticism. *If* I still have friends now, I have them—how to put it?—***in spite of*** what I am or would like to

become. And so *you*, dear venerated friend, have remained kind to me and I hope with all my heart that I will be able to thank you *for that* and cultivate in my garden a fruit that is to *your liking*." Letter of January 1, 1883, eKGWB/BVN-1883,367. My trans.

7. *Ecce Homo*, chap. titled "Things Human, All Too Human," § 5, eKGWB/EH-MA-5. Trans. Kaufmann in *On the Genealogy of Morals* and *Ecce Homo*, 288. Trans. mod.

8. *On the Genealogy of Morals*, Preface, § 2, eKGWB/GM-Vorrede-2. Trans. Kaufmann in *On the Genealogy of Morals* and *Ecce Homo*, 15–16. Trans. mod.

9. Posthumous fragment eKGWB/NF-1876,23[159]. My trans.

10. Meysenbug, *Stimmungsbilder*, 86. My trans.

11. Malwida to Olga Monod-Herzen, April 29, 1877, in *Breife von und an Malwida von Meysenbug*, 141–42. My trans. On Rée, his relationship with Nietzsche, and type of philosophy in which he was interested, see: Hubert Treiber's introduction to Paul Rée, *Gesammelte Werke, 1875–1885* (Berlin/New York: de Gruyter, 2004); Paul-Laurent Assoun's study-preface to Paul Rée, *De l'origine des sentiments moraux* (Paris: PUF, 1982); and Maria Cristina Fornari, *La morale evolutiva del gregge. Nietzsche legge Spencer e Mill* (Pisa: ETS, 2006).

12. This is the title of aphorism 136 in *Things Human, All Too Human*, except that Rée reverses the order of the terms of the original title—instead of "Von der christlichen Askese und Heiligkeit"—*Of Christian asceticism and holiness*—which is the title of Nietzsche's aphorism, Rée has "Der christlichen Heiligkeit und Askese." —Trans.

13. Rée to Nietzsche, May 10, 1878, KGB II/6/2, 852-853. My trans.

14. *Cosima Wagner's Diaries, Volume Two: 1878–1883*, ed. Martin Gregor-Dellin and Dietrich Mack, trans. Geoffrey Skelton (New York, London: Harcourt Brace Jovanovich, 1980), June 24, 1878, 100. See also the following dates: April 25, 29, 30; May 23, 28, 30; June 9, 26, 27, 28, 29, 30; July 1, 3, 21, 27 and August 2, 1878, as well as January 28, 1879.

15. Letter quoted in Moulin-Eckart, *Cosima Wagner*, vol. II, 742.

16. Rohde to Nietzsche, June 16, 1878, KGB II/6/2, 895-896. My trans.

17. Rohde had particularly appreciated the parts concerning Greek civilization.

18. Nietzsche to Rohde, shortly after June 16, 1878, eKGWB/BVN-1878,727. My trans. And yet, was it not with his inseparable friend Erwin Rohde that Nietzsche had planned in 1869 to spend a year in Paris, studying chemistry? "I had truly wanted, once again, before being tied by the chains of a profession, I had ardently desired to glory in the profound seriousness and the magical enchantment of an itinerant life and, once more, to savor the indescribable bliss of being a spectator and not an actor, in the company of my most faithful and appreciative of friends. I imagined the two of us, with earnest eyes and smiling lips, striding through the Parisian crowd, a pair of philosopher *flâneurs* that people would grow accustomed to seeing everywhere together, at the museums and in the libraries, at the Closerie des Lilas and at Notre Dame, carrying the seriousness of their thought and the tender appreciation of their mutual solidarity everywhere. And what must I trade for such vagrancy, for such friendly proximity? [. . .] Alas, we are truly the fools of fate: even last week, I wanted to write to you to propose that we study chemistry together and send philology where it belongs, among the household goods of the forefathers. And now the demon 'fate' elicits me with a professorship in philology." Nietzsche to Rohde, January 16, 1869, eKGWB/BVN-1869,608. My trans.

19. Cf. the letters from Nietzsche to Rohde: May 19, 23, November 11, 1887, eKGWB/BVN-1887, 848, 852, 950; and January 4, 1889, eKGWB/BVN-1889,1250.

20. Mathilde Maier to Nietzsche, early July, 1878, KGB II/6/2, 910–14. My trans.

21. Nietzsche to Mathilde Maier, July 15, 1878, eKGWB/BVN-1878,734. My trans.

22. Things Human, All Too Human, aph. 13, eKGWB/MA-13. Trans. Hollingdale in Human, All Too Human, 17. Trans. mod. For an analysis of this aphorism, see at least Peter Heller, *Von den ersten und letzten Dingen. Studien und Kommentar zu einer Aphorismenreihe von Friedrich Nietzsche* (Berlin: de Gruyter, 1972), 153–62 and Hubert Treiber, "Zur 'Logik des Traums' bei Nietzsche. Anmerkungen zu den Traumaphorismen aus MA," *Nietzsche-Studien*, 23 (1994), 1–41.

23. "Glockenlaute—goldenes Licht durch die Fenster. Traum. Ursache a posteriori hineingedichtet wie bei den Augenempfindungen," eKGWB/NF-1876,21[38], facsimile DFGA/N-II-3, 36. My trans.

24. Brenner to his family, December 27, 1876, in Stummann-Bowert, 211–12. My trans.

25. Posthumous fragment 6[77] 1859, in KGW I/2, 104; this last reference is signaled in KGW IV/4, 169. My trans.

26. "In windstillen halbdunklen Gängen gehen, während über uns die Bäume von heftigen Winden bewegt rauschen, in hellerem Schein," KGW IV/4, 210, facsimile DFGA/N-II-3,15. My trans.

27. Nietzsche to Seydlitz, end of February 1877, eKGWB/BVN-1877,599. My trans.

28. *Things Human, All Too Human*, aph. 275, eKGWB/MA-275. Trans. Hollingdale in *Human, All Too Human*, 129–30. See Renate Müller-Buck, 431–32, who quotes a letter from Heinrich Köselitz and Paul Widemann to Nietzsche of July 31, 1877, which contains a description of Brenner's skeptical and cynical nature.

29. *Things Human, All Too Human*, aph. 478, eKGWB/MA-478. Trans. Hollingdale in *Human, All Too Human*, 176–77. Trans. mod. In the draft, instead of "Craftsman in the South," Nietzsche had written "Craftsmen here"—that is, in Sorrento, cf. KGW IV/4, 229, facsimile DFGA/U-II-5, 31.

30. Malwida to Olga Monod-Herzen, Thursday (before April 10, 1877), in *Briefe von und an Malwida von Meysenbug*, 127–28. My trans. "Long live Mary's heart, long live God who loves her so"; Malwida writes "Eviva" instead of "Evviva" and "amà" instead of "ama."

31. Posthumous fragments eKGWB/NF-1878,28[10] and 27[97]. My trans. Facsimile DFGA/N-II-6,5; Nietzsche writes "que" instead of "che."

32. *Assorted Opinions and Maxims*, aph. 171, eKGWB/VM-171. Trans. Hollingdale in *Human, All Too Human*, 253; the draft can be found in Sorrento manuscript Mp XIV 1, 103.

33. Posthumous fragments eKGWB/NF-1876,16[50], 16[52], and 17[39]. My trans. Facsimiles DFGA/N-II-1,241 and 244, DFGA/U-II-5,165.

34. *Things Human, All Too Human*, aph. 291, eKGWB/MA-291. Trans. Hollingdale in *Human, All Too Human*, 134. Trans. mod.

35. See the accounts of Malwida, of Brenner, and of Nietzsche himself, chap. 2.

36. Nietzsche to Heinrich Köselitz, August 16, 1883, eKGWB/BVN-1883,452. My trans.

37. In retrospect, Zarathustra will say: "[I]n the marketplace one convinces with gestures. But reasons make the mob mistrustful." *Thus Spoke Zarathustra*, IV, "On the Higher Man," § 9, eKGWB/Za-IV-Menschen-9. Trans. Kaufmann, 290.

38. *Thus Spoke Zarathustra*, I, "Zarathustra's prologue," § 9, eKGWB/Za-I-Vorrede-9. Trans. Kaufmann, 24.

39. Nietzsche's texts and manuscripts show how *Thus Spoke Zarathustra* was composed in large part by condensing the aphorisms of previous books, especially from the period of the philosophy of the free spirit. Nietzsche explicitly says this, moreover, in a letter to Malwida around April 20, 1883: "In fact, I 'committed' the stunt (and the folly) of writing the *commentaries* before the text. —But *who* has *read* them? I mean: studied them for years?" eKGWB/BVN-1883,404; he reiterates this to Overbeck on April 7, 1884: "I reread 'Daybreak' and 'The Gay Science' in their entirety and found, incidentally, that there is almost no single line that cannot serve as an introduction, a preparation, and a commentary to Zarathustra. It is a *fact* that I wrote the commentary before the *text*—" eKGWB/BVN-1884,504. My trans. He repeats this a third time to Resa von Schirnhofer, early May, 1884, eKGWB/BVN-1884,510.

40. Posthumous fragment eKGWB/NF-1888, 14 [61]. My trans.

41. Nietzsche uses the French term.

42. Nietzsche uses the French term.

43. Posthumous fragment eKGWB/NF-1888,15[67]. My trans.

44. Posthumous fragment eKGWB/NF-1888,16[7]. My trans.

45. *Thus Spoke Zarathustra*, "On the Gift-Giving Virtue," § 1, eKGWB/Za-I-Tugend-1. Trans. Kaufmann, 76.

46. *Thus Spoke Zarathustra*, "On the Gift-Giving Virtue," § 2, eKGWB/Za-I-Tugend-2. Trans. Kaufmann, 76.

47. *Thus Spoke Zarathustra*, "On the Gift-Giving Virtue," § 3, eKGWB/Za-I-Tugend-3. Trans. Kaufmann, 78.

48. Köselitz to Nietzsche, July 24, 1883, KGB III/2, 383.

49. Nietzsche to Köselitz, August 3, 1883, eKGWB/BVN-1883,446. My trans. At that time, Köselitz was in Venice.

50. *Thus Spoke Zarathustra*, II, "The Child with the Mirror," eKGWB/Za-II-Kind. Trans. Kaufmann, 84.

51. *Thus Spoke Zarathustra*, II, "The Dancing Song," eKGWB/Za-II-Tanzlied. Trans. Kaufmann, 108. Trans. mod.

52. Posthumous fragment eKGWB/NF-1883,16 [89]. My trans.

53. *Thus Spoke Zarathustra*, III, "On Involuntary Bliss," eKGWB/Za-III-Seligkeit. Trans. Kaufmann, 161–62. Trans. mod. It is not by chance that, in the preface to a work dedicated to the eternal return, Nietzsche claims to have no other audience than "this ideal community, which Zarathustra cultivated on the blessed isles," eKGWB/NF-1884,26[244]. My trans.

54. *Thus Spoke Zarathustra*, IV, "The Cry of Distress," eKGWB/Za-IV-Nothschrei. Trans. Kaufmann, 243.

55. Posthumous fragment eKGWB/NF-1883,15[17]. My trans. Cf. also: 20[80], 22[4], and eKGWB/NF-1884,29[23].

56. *Thus Spoke Zarathustra*, IV, "The Cry of Distress," eKGWB/Za-IV-Nothschrei. Trans. Kaufmann, 243.

57. Giuliano Campioni has emphasized the relationship between the fourth part of *Zarathustra* and the figures of European decadence analyzed in Paul Bourget's *Essais de psychologie*

contemporaine, cf. Campioni, "'Der höhere Mensch' nach dem Tod Gottes," *Nietzsche-Studien*, 28 (1999), 336–55, and Campioni, *Les lectures françaises de Nietzsche* (Paris: PUF, 2001), 187ff.

58. *Thus Spoke Zarathustra*, IV, "The Welcome," eKGWB/Za-IV-Begrüssung. Trans. Kaufmann, 281–82.

59. *Thus Spoke Zarathustra*, IV, "The Welcome," eKGWB/Za-IV-Begrüssung. Trans. Kaufmann, 282–83. Trans. mod.

60. *Thus Spoke Zarathustra*, IV, "The Sign," eKGWB/Za-IV-Begrüssung. Trans. Kaufmann, 326.

61. Cf. Homer, *Odyssey*, IV, 5651–586, and Hesiod, *Works and Days*, 166–73.

62. I have given only a few limited references to the works of Hesiod: Nietzsche spoke of the blessed isles to his students in a course on *Works and Days,* which he held several times, from 1869 to 1876, and for the last time during the semester preceding his departure for Sorrento (see the notebooks kept by his students, published in KGW II/2, 369, 371; cf. Andrea Bollinger and Franziska Trenkle, *Nietzsche in Basel* (Basel: Schwabe, 2000), 71–79). In his personal library, Nietzsche had two copies of Hesiod's Greek text *Hesiodea quake feruntur carmina* (Lipsiæ: Teubneri, 1870). In the copy that now bears the shelf mark C 43, verses 156–74, where the blessed isles are spoken of (85–86), are signaled by a series of crosses drawn at the start of each verse; in the copy bearing the shelf mark C 107, some of these verses are underlined and philologically commentated on. Nietzsche uses the Homeric and Hesiodean expression about the isles at the edges of the world in two letters to Köselitz, in March and April of 1882, eKGWB/BVN-1882,208 and 220.

63. Nietzsche to Erwin Rohde, December 15, 1870, eKGWB/BVN-1870,113. My trans.

64. Posthumous fragment eKGWB/NF-1880,6. My trans. On the isle as a meeting place for a society of thinkers, see aphorism 314 of *Daybreak*: "In the midst of the ocean of becoming we awake on a little island no bigger than a boat, we adventurers and birds of passage, and look around us for a few moments [. . .] in this little space, we find other birds of passage and hear of others still who have been here before—and thus we live a precarious minute of knowing and divining," eKGWB/M-314. Trans. Hollingdale in *Daybreak: Thoughts on the Prejudices of Morality* (Cambridge: Cambridge University Press, 1997), 157–58. Trans. mod.

65. *Ecce Homo*, chap. titled "Things Human, All Too Human," § 2, eKGWB/EH-MA-2. Trans. Kaufmann in *On the Genealogy of Morals* and *Ecce Homo*, 284.

66. "Auf vulkanischem Boden gedeiht alles." Posthumous fragment eKGWB/NF-1876,21[12]. My trans. This fragment seems to be derived from Wilhelm C. Fuchs, *Vulkane und Erdbeben* (Leipzig: Brockhaus, 1875), 13, where we read that at the foot of Mount Etna "die üppigste Vegetation auch im Winter gedeiht." In this book, which Nietzsche had bought in November 1875 and had bound in January 1876, he could find a whole series of details on Vesuvius and on the volcanic nature of the isle of Ischia.

67. "Prehistoric eras are defined by tradition: during vast periods of time, nothing happens. In historical time, the determining fact is always a separation from tradition, a difference of opinion—it is *free thought* that makes history. The faster the reversal of opinions takes place, the faster the world runs, the chronicle transforms into a newspaper, and, finally, the telegraph assesses how the opinions of men have changed within hours." Posthumous fragment eKGWB/NF-1876,19[89]. My trans.

68. *Thus Spoke Zarathustra*, "On Great Events," eKGWB/Za-II-Ereignisse. Trans. Kaufmann, 129. On the literary and scientific sources of this chapter, see Andler, *Nietzsche*, 259; Hubert Treiber, "Beiträge zur Quelenforschung," *Nietzsche-Studien*, 27 (1998), 562, and KGW VI/6, 891.

69. Trans. Kaufmann in *Thus Spoke Zarathustra*, 131.

70. Posthumous fragments eKGWB/NF-1883,10 [28] and [29]. My trans.

71. *Thus Spoke Zarathustra*, "On Great Events," eKGWB/Za-II-Ereignisse. Trans. Kaufmann, 131. Trans. mod.

72. *Thus Spoke Zarathustra*, "The Stillest Hour," eKGWB/Za-II-Stunde. Trans. Kaufmann, 146.

73. *Thus Spoke Zarathustra*, "On Great Events," eKGWB/Za-II-Ereignisse. Trans. Kaufmann, 132.

CHAPTER FIVE

1. Nietzsche to Rée, April 17, 1877, eKGWB/BVN-1877,606. My trans.

2. Nietzsche to Elisabeth, April 25, 1877, eKGWB/BVN-1877,609. My trans.

3. Nietzsche to Overbeck, May 7, 1877, eKGWB/BVN-1877,612. My trans.

4. Notebook N II 8, *Notizkalender für das Jahr 1877*. My trans. On the question of the black fez that Nietzsche had received as a Christmas gift, cf. the letter from Elizabeth to Nietzsche of December 19 (KGB II/6/1, 460) and Nietzsche's response of December 30, 1876, eKGWB/BVN-1876,583.

5. Malwida too had vision problems.

6. Nietzsche to Malwida, May 13, 1877, eKGWB/BVN-1877,615. My trans.

7. Seydlitz to Nietzsche, May 16, 1877, KGB II/6/1, 556. My trans.

8. Malwida to Nietzsche, May 17, 1877, KGB II/6/1, 557. My trans.

9. Mazzino Montinari, *Nietzsche* (Paris: PUF, 2001), 9. My trans.

10. Notebook N II 2, 4, facsimile DFGA/N-II-2, 4; the transcription of the two fragments can be found in KGW IV/4, 451, 240. My trans. I have devoted two studies to the motif of the bells of Genoa: "Aucune des choses humaines n'est digne de grand sérieux," *Œvres et critique*, XXV, 1, Tübingen, 2000, 107–23, and "Les cloches du nihilisme et l'éternel retour du même," in Jean-François Mattéi, ed., *Nietzsche et le temps des nihilismes* (Paris: PUF, 2005), 191–208. See also Olivier Ponton, *Philosophie de la légèreté*, 46–81.

11. As Joyce will later write in *A Portrait of the Artist as a Young Man* (New York: Huebsch, 1916), 205. The conserved epiphanies have been published by Hans Walter Gabler in the fourth volume of *The James Joyce Archive* (New York: Garland Publishing, 1978).

12. James Joyce, *Stephen Hero* (New York: New Directions, 1944), 211.

13. *Ibid.*, 213.

14. Walter H. Pater, *The Renaissance. Studies in Art and Poetry* (London: Macmillan, 1877); Gabriele D'Annunzio, *Il fuoco* (Milano: Treves, 1900). Umberto Eco underlined the debt to Walter Pater and was the first to reveal the origin of the term *epiphany* in D'Annunzio, cf. Umberto Eco, *Le poetiche di Joyce* (Milano: Bompiani, 2002), 44–45 and 49–50.

15. Joyce, *A Portrait*, 250.

16. James Joyce, *Ulysses*, ed. Hans Walter Gabler (New York: Random House, 1986), 34. According to Franco Moretti, the concept of the epiphany returns even in *Ulysses*, in the paradoxical form of the commonplace. These commonplaces, indeed, receive a minimum of meaning whose return, with small variations, prevents the total disintegration of the metropolitan man: "commonplaces are *Bloom's epiphanies*." Cf. Franco Moretti, *Modern Epic: The World System from Goethe to García Márquez*, trans. Quintin Hoare (London, New York: Verso, 1996), 163.

17. Joyce, *Finnegans Wake*, IV, 626. Cf. Fritz Senn, *Joyce's Dislocutions: Essays on Reading as Translation* (Baltimore and London: Johns Hopkins University Press, 1984); Giovanni Melchiori, *Joyce: il mestiere dello scrittore* (Torino: Einaudi, 1994), 4–6, 216.

18. *Things Human, All Too Human*, aph. 586, eKGWB/MA-586. Trans. Hollingdale in *Human, All Too Human*, 189.

19. Cf. posthumous fragments eKGWB/NF-1875,11[11] and eKGWB/NF-1878,28[8], [9], [6]. Nietzsche's childhood memories have been commented on by Montinari in *Nietzsche lesen*, 22–37. On the subject of butterflies as a metaphor for happiness, but also of the fragility of thought and the lightness of literary and philosophical creation, I refer the reader to my article "Les pensées papillons," *Genesis* 22 (2003), 7–11. The reproduction in facsimile of the notebook titled *Memorabilia* can be consulted in DFGA/N-II-6.

20. Posthumous fragment eKGWB/NF-1878,28[18]. My trans.

21. Without using the word epiphany, Montinari had already pointed out that Nietzsche's writings "are all born of 'spiritual dispositions' that are very often overwhelming," *Nietzsche*, 21. My trans.

22. *On the Genealogy of Morals*, II, § 12, eKGWB/GM-II-12. Trans. Kaufmann in *On the Genealogy of Morals* and *Ecce Homo*, 78.

23. Joyce, *A Portrait*, 250.

24. Posthumous fragment 15[41] 1863, KGW I/3, 190. My trans.

25. Posthumous fragment 4[77] 1858, KGW I/1, 283. My trans. A fleeting note on the pleasure he experienced as a child when he heard the peal of the bells can also be found in one of the philosopher's notebooks: "The shiver of pleasure at the sound of the bells," eKGWB/NF-1880,6 [172]. My trans.

26. Posthumous fragments 5[1] 1858, KGW I/2, 3; 4[77] 1858, KGW I/1, 286; 10[10] 1861, KGW I/2, 26off. My trans.

27. Posthumous fragment 6[18] 1859, KGW I/2, 53. My trans. This image is also used in a collection of six poems of September 1862 (13[22] 1862, KGW I/2, 467). The bell also resounds in another poem of this collection, titled "Despair" (466).

28. Nietzsche to his mother, November 25, 1860, eKGWB/BVN-1860,193. My trans. Every year at Pforta, on the night before the Day of the Dead, homage was paid to the memory of the students that had died the year before, cf. KGW I/IV, 137.

29. Posthumous fragment 14[29] 1862, KGW I/3, 57.

30. Friedrich Schiller, "Das Lied von der Glocke"(1800): lines 244ff: "Von dem Dome / Schwer und bang / Tönt die Glocke / Grabgesang," where the three vowels "o, e, a" alternate, imitating the piercing sound of the death knell. My trans. Nietzsche had been familiar with this famous poem by Schiller at least since the celebration of the poet's centenary at Pforta in 1859, when he had participated as a chorus boy in the performance of the poem as a cantata,

over music composed by Andreas Romburg, cf. posthumous fragment 7 [3] 1859 (KGW I/3, 175) and the letter to his mother of mid-November 1859, eKGWB/BVN-1859,114. Paul Deussen recalls that he recited Schiller's "Song of the Bell" in Pforta while Nietzsche improvised a piano accompaniment: Paul Deussen, *Erinnerungen an Friedrich Nietzsche* (Leipzig: F. A. Brockhaus, 1901), 17.

31. Goethe, "Epilog zu Schillers Glocke" (1805), lines 9ff. My trans. Goethe's "Epilogue" was, naturally, also included in the celebration in Schiller's honor; Nietzsche quotes from it later in the posthumous text, *On the Future of our Educational Institutions*, § I and IV (eKGWB/ BA-I and IV), in the first *Untimely Meditation*, § 4 (eKGWB/DS-4), and in a note of 1879: "I have to cry when I read Goethe's words for Schiller: 'and behind him the fragile appearance, etc.' Why?" eKGWB/NF-1879,41[68]. My trans.

32. Cf. Lord Byron, *Die beiden Foscari*, in *Sämmtliche Werke* (Leipzig: Wigand, 1864), end of act V, 85–87; Nietzsche, posthumous fragments 12[4] 1861, KGW I/2, 347 and 16[2] 1863– 1864, KGW I/3, 238. My trans.

33. Heinrich Heine, *Über die französische Bühne. Vertraute Briefe an August Lewald*, in *Säm-mtliche Werke* (Homburg: Hoffmann und Campe, 1862), vol. I, 133. My trans. Nietzsche quotes this work in a letter to Rohde on October 8, 1868, eKGWB/BVN-1868,591.

34. Schiller, "Das Lied von der Glocke," lines 403ff. My trans.

35. Plato, *The Laws*, 803b–d in Plato, *Dialogi Secundum Thrasylli tetralogias dispositi* (Lipsiæ: Teubneri, 1862). My trans. Several pages earlier (644d), Plato had written: "Let us suppose that each of us living creatures is a puppet constructed by the gods, we do not know whether it is as a plaything for them or to some serious end, but we do know that these sensa-tions inside us are like sinews or cords that drag us along and, being opposed to each other, pull us to opposite actions; and here it is that lies the line dividing virtue and vice." My trans.

36. Arthur Schopenhauer, *Parerga und Paralipomena,* in *Sämtliche Werke* (Leipzig: Brock-haus, 1874), vol. I, 435. My trans.

37. Cf. Albert Brenner's letter of December 4, 1876: "In the evening, Dr. Rée reads aloud. He has already read Jakob Burckhardt's lessons on history (in manuscript) and those of Thu-cydides. Now we are reading *The Laws* of Plato," in Stummann-Bowert, 210. My trans.

38. "*Alles Menschliche insgesamt ist keines grossen Ernstes werth*" is written on page 64 of notebook N II 3, facsimile DFGA/N-II-3,64.

39. "Über den Rhythmus (1875)," in Nietzsche, *Gesammelte Werke* (München: Musarion-ausgabe, 1922), 5: 475–76. My trans. The passage of Plato is also quoted in the fragment eK-GWB/NF-1875, 9 in a different context.

40. Nietzsche had discussed Leopardi's pessimism in the second *Untimely Meditation*, § 1 (eKGWB/HL-1): "Nothing is worth your moving. / Earth is unworthy of your sighs. Life / is bitterness and boredom, nothing more. / And the world is foul. / Now be still" (from the poem "To Himself"). Trans. William Arrowsmith in *Unmodern Observations*, ed. and trans. William Arrowsmith (New Haven: Yale University Press, 1990), 93.

41. The note quoted above is found on page 19 of notebook N II 2 (facsimile in DFGA/N-II-2, 19). My trans. It is the first draft of aphorism 113 of *Things Human, All Too Human,* eKGWB/ MA-113. Trans. Hollingdale in *Human, All Too Human*, 65–66. Trans. mod. In his response, Wagner relies heavily on this aphorism to challenge the historical critique which, pervaded

by Judaism, does not know the true ideal figure of the Savior: "Who knows Jesus? —Perhaps the historical critique? It belongs to Judaism and is amazed that even still today on Sunday morning, the church bells ring for a Jew crucified 2,000 years ago, exactly as all Jews are amazed at this" (Wagner, *Sämtliche Schriften und Dichtung* (Leipzig: Breitkof & Härtel, 1991), vol. 10, 141).

42. "Kindisch und schaurig und wehmutsvoll / klang die Weise der Zeit mir oft: / sehet nun sing ich ihr Lied? / hört, ob das Glockenspiel / nicht sich verwandelt in Glockenernst / oder ob es klingt / hoch herab wie vom Genua-Thurm / Kindisch jedoch ach schaurig / Schaurig und wehmutsvoll," eKGWB/NF-1877,22[45]. My trans.

43. Facsimile in DFGA/Mp-XIV-1,222; the first note is transcribed in KGW IV/4, 240, the second is fragment eKGWB/NF-1877,23[188]. My trans. See also fragment eKGWB/NF-1877, 22[197].

44. Nietzsche's copy is conserved in the Herzogin Anna Amalia Bibliothek of Weimar, under the shelf mark C 63-b; the underlining can be found on page 298. It is one of the very rare underlinings to appear in this volume.

45. Facsimile in DFGA/Mp-XIV-1,114. My trans.

46. *Epilogue* is, of course, also an allusion to Goethe's "Epilogue" to Schiller's "Song of the Bell."

47. Elisabetta Mengaldo, "Strategie di reticenza e demistificazione: il trattino di sospensione negli aforismi di Friedrich Nietzsche," *Studi germanici*, 1–2 (2005), 25–48. On the use of this typographical character and, more generally, on the forms of aposiopesis in Nietzsche and the influence of the French moralists and Laurence Sterne, see Vivetta Vivarelli's analysis (Vivarelli 1998, 159ff. and 25ff.), which quotes, among others, the fragment eKGWB/NF-1885,34[147], in which Nietzsche declares that he prefers his em dashes to his fully formulated thoughts.

48. This interpretation reinforces Andler's accurate observations concerning the translation of the title *Menschliches, Allzumenschliches* into Neo-Latin languages: "I am aware that well-known translators, and blindly after them, the totality of French critics, translate *Menschliches, Allzumenschliches* as *Humain, trop humain* (*Human, All Too Human*). They translate as if Nietzsche had written *Menschlich, Allzumenschlich*. But Nietzsche added an inflection, and we must, therefore, translate it. *Menschliches, Allzumenschliches* are substantives in the partitive form. *Menschlich, Allzumenschlich* would be adjectives in an attributive function. It is a misinterpretation to confuse these two functions. Nietzsche, who often thought in Latin, could have called his book *Humana, Nimis Humana*. We do not have the right to translate it as if he had said *Humanum, Nimis Humanum*" (Andler, *Nietzsche*, vol. 2, 321–22, n. My trans.) We add that, in order to read it philosophically, we must take yet another step backwards and read it in Greek, as a reference and a response to Plato's human things (τῶν ἀνθρωπίνων) without value.

49. *Things Human, All Too Human*, eKGWB/MA-638. Trans. Hollingdale in *Human, All Too Human*, 204.

50. Nietzsche to Rohde, February 22, 1884, eKGWB/BVN-1884,490. My trans.

51. *Things Human, All Too Human*, eKGWB/MA-638. Trans. Hollingdale in *Human, All Too Human*, 203.

52. *Thus Spoke Zarathustra*, II, "Upon the Blessed Isles," eKGWB/Za-II-Inseln. Trans. Kaufmann, 85.

53. Nietzsche takes up the image from Hölderlin's *Empedocles*, in which the ripe fruit represents the protagonist's teaching: "Today is my autumn day and the fruit falls / of itself," cf. Friedrich Hölderlin, *Empedocles*, lines 1514–15. The image of the ripe fruit that falls from the tree can also be found in a letter of 1869: "Outside, before my windows lies thoughtful autumn in the clear, soft sunlight, Nordic autumn, which I love as much as my very best friends, because it is so ripe and unconsciously without desire. The fruit falls from the tree without a gust of wind." Nietzsche to Rohde, October 7, 1869, eKGWB/BVN-1869,33. My trans. Cf. Vivetta Vivarelli, *L'immagine rovesciata: le letture di Nietzsche* (Genova: Matietti, 1992), 154ff. The image of the fig tree also contains a parodic counterpoint of the Gospels, in the passage where Jesus, "[seeing] a fig tree by the road, [. . .] went up to it but found nothing on it except leaves. Then he said to it, 'May you never bear fruit again!' Immediately the tree withered" (Gospel of Matthew 21, 19).

54. Ralph Waldo Emerson, *Die Führung des Lebens. Gedanken und Studien* (Leipzig: Steinacker, 1862), 185, which Nietzsche used in his first philosophical writings of 1862, on fate, history, and freedom, and which he never ceased to reread. Cf. Benedetta Zavatta, *La sfida del carattere. Nietzsche lettore di Emerson* (Roma: Editori Riuniti, 2006), particularly 40ff., and Vivarelli, *L'immagine rovesciata*, 152–53.

55. *Thus Spoke Zarathustra*, III, "Before Sunrise," eKGWB/Za-III-Sonnen. Trans. Kaufmann, 165–66. "Let us note that 'By Chance' translates the expression '*von Ohngefähr*,' which sounds like a noble title (particle *von*). Cf. in the Bible, *Wisdom* 2.2, where we read—in Luther's translation—with the same expression: 'we are born by chance,'" Mazzino Montinari, critical apparatus to *Thus Spoke Zarathustra*, in *Opere di Friedrich Nietzsche*, tome VI/1 (Milano: Adelphi, 1968), 465.

56. Cf. Emerson, chapter on "Nature" of *Versuche* (Hannover: Carl Meyer, 1858), 391–92; Nietzsche to Gersdorff, April 7, 1866, eKGWB/BVN-1866,500. My trans. Arthur Schopenhauer, *Die Welt als Wille und Vorstellung*, in *Sämtliche Werke* (Leipzig: Brockhaus, 1873), § 34. The Emersonian image is also found in the fragment eKGWB/NF-1879, 45 [1].

57. *Thus Spoke Zarathustra*, IV, "At Noon," eKGWB/Za-IV-Mittags. Trans. Kaufmann, 276–77. The connection between noon and happiness was also present in aphorism 308 of *The Wanderer and His Shadow* (eKGWB/WS-308) and will reappear in the dithyramb "The Sun Sinks" of *Dithyrambs of Dionysus* (eKGWB/DD-Sonne-1). On the Greek sources, see, for example, Karl Schlechta, *Nietzsche grosser Mittag* (Frankfurt: Klostermann, 1954), 34ff.

58. *Thus Spoke Zarathustra*, III, "The Other Dancing Song," eKGWB/Za-III-Tanzlied-2. Trans. Kaufmann, 226–27.

59. *Thus Spoke Zarathustra*, III, "The Other Dancing Song," eKGWB/Za-III-Tanzlied-3. Trans. Kaufmann, 227–28. Trans. mod. As Peter André Bloch has pointed out ("'Aus meinem Leben.' Der selbstporträtcharakter von Nietzsches frühen Lebensbeschreibungen: Selbstdialog als Selbstbefragung," *Nietzscheforschung*, 2 [1995], 70, n.), the metrics of Zarathustra's round are constructed so as to imitate the sound of the bells: "Oh Mensch! Gieb Acht! / Was spricht die tiefe Mitternacht? / 'Ich schlief, ich schlief —, / 'Aus tiefem Traum bin ich erwacht: —.'" Moreover, it is said in the drafts that Zarathustra "counted the strokes of the midnight bell and willingly rhymed them in his song," eKGWB/NF-1884,31[64]. My trans. It is regrettable that Mahler did not take account of this when he put this text to music in his third symphony.

60. "The words of the Preacher, the son of David, king in Jerusalem. Vanity of vanities, saith the Preacher, vanity of vanities; all *is* vanity. [. . .] The thing that hath been, it *is that* which shall be; and that which is done *is* that which shall be done: and *there is* no new *thing* under the sun. [. . .] I have seen all the works that are done under the sun; and, behold, all *is* vanity and vexation of spirit." *The Holy Bible: King James Version*, 2000, Ecclesiastes: 1, 2, 9, 14.

61. See the little moral book, *Dialogue Between an Almanac Seller and a Passerby*, in Giacomo Leopardi, *Operette morali* (Torino: Loescher, 1993). Trans. Charles Edwardes in *Essays and Dialogues of Giacomo Leopardi* (Boston: J. R. Osgood and Co., 1882), 179ff. From one century to the other, from the pessimism of the eighteenth century to the decadent literature of the nineteenth century, Nietzsche will rediscover this type of reasoning in the works of other authors, and, for example, in his copy of the *Journal des Goncourt*, he will underline the following passage: "It is impossible to find a man who would like to relive his life. One can hardly find a woman who would want to relive her eighteenth year. That is the judge of life," Edmond and Jules Huot de Goncourt, *Journal des Goncourt. Mémoires de la vie littéraire* (Paris: Charpentier, 1887), 193 (May 1, 1864). My trans. Nietzsche's copy of the book is conserved at the Herzogin Anna Amalia Bibliothek of Weimar, shelf mark C 550-a. Partial English translation, *Pages from the Goncourt Journals*, trans. Robert Baldick (New York: New York Review Books Classics, 2006).

62. Arthur Schopenhauer, *Die Welt als Wille und Vorstellung*, vol. 1, § 59, vol. 2, § XLI. Trans. E. F. J. Payne in *The World as Will and Representation* (New York: Dover Publications, 1969), 1: 324 and 2: 465.

63. Eduard von Hartmann, *Philosophie des Unbewussten. Versuch einer Weltanschauung* (Berlin: Carl Duncker's Verlag, 1869), 534. Trans. Frank Chouraqui in D'Iorio, "The Eternal Return: Genesis and Interpretation," *The Agonist* 4, no. 1 (*Nietzsche Circle*, Spring 2011), 12–13. Trans. mod.

64. *The Gay Science*, aphorism 341, eKGWB/FW-341. Trans. Kaufmann in *The Gay Science* (New York: Vintage Books, 1974), 273–74.

65. Ludwig Boltzmann, *Vorlesungen über Gastheorie* (Leipzig: Barth, 1896–1898), vol. II, § 90, 256–59; cf. Paolo D'Iorio, *La linea e il circolo. Cosmologia e filosofia dell'eterno ritorno in Nietzsche* (Genova: Pantograf, 1995), 362ff., and D'Iorio, "Nietzsche et l'éternel retour. Genèse et interpretation," *Nietzsche*, Cahiers de l'Herne (Paris: l'Herne, 2000), 361–89, English trans. "The Eternal Return: Genesis and Interpretation."

66. As Gilles Deleuze asserts, on the contrary, "Conclusions. Sur la volonté de puissance et l'éternel retour," in Deleuze, ed., *Nietzsche. Actes du colloque de Royaumont du 4 au 8 juillet 1964* (Paris: Les éditions de Minuit, 1967), 284.

67. The fact that the ugliest man represents the historical sense (and the killer of God) is confirmed by the drafts for the fourth part of *Zarathustra*: eKGWB/NF-1884,25[101], 31[10], 32 [4].

68. *Thus Spoke Zarathustra*, IV, "The Sleepwalker's Song," § 1, eKGWB/Za-IV-Nachtwandler-1. Trans. Kaufmann, 317–18. Kaufmann translates the title of this parable as "The Drunken Song," which corresponds to the title that Nietzsche wrote on his copy of *Thus Spoke Zarathustra*. Yet the printed title is "Das Nachtwandler-Lied," which literally translates to "The Sleepwalker-Song" or "The Somnambulist-Song." Following the guidance of the author, I have translated this title accordingly in the present text. —Trans.

69. *Thus Spoke Zarathustra*, IV, "The Sleepwalker's Song," § 6, eKGWB/Za-IV-Nachtwandler-6. Trans. Kaufmann, 321. Trans. mod.

70. Arthur Schopenhauer, *Die Welt als Wille und Vorstellung*, vol. 1, § 58. Trans. E. F. J Payne in *The World as Will and Representation*, 1: 321–22.

71. *Thus Spoke Zarathustra*, II, "On Priests," eKGWB/Za-II-Priester. Trans. Kaufmann, 92. Trans. mod.

72. *Thus Spoke Zarathustra*, IV, "The Sleepwalker's Song," § 6, eKGWB/Za-IV-Nachtwandler-6. Trans. Kaufmann, 321.

73. Let us point out that in the draft of the manuscript, Nietzsche had written *Sterb-Glück*, then, in the final draft, he removes the hyphen and adds the "e" of the dative case to create the compound *Sterbeglücke* on the model of *Sterbeglocke* (cf. notebook Z II 9, 12, transcribed in KGW VI/4, 791).

74. Cf. notebook Z II 9, 26, transcribed in KGW VI/4, 793.

75. Johann Wolfgang von Goethe, *Faust*, "Study," lines 1698 ff. My trans.

76. *Thus Spoke Zarathustra*, IV, "The Sleepwalker's Song," § 10, eKGWB/Za-IV-Nachtwandler-10. Trans. Kaufmann, 323.

77. The phrase "now the world is perfect" was also written in a provisional version of the sixth paragraph (cf. notebook Z II 9, 12, transcribed in KGW VI/4, 791), but Nietzsche later eliminated it, probably in order to better calibrate the crescendo so as to reach the union of midnight and noon only in the tenth paragraph.

78. Among other references in this text, let us recall that Nietzsche reverses the antithesis between day and night contained in Wagner's *Tristan and Isolde*. Communion with the whole does not come about in a metaphysical, nocturnal dimension through amorous passion that pushes one to the loss of individuality as in *Tristan* (and as in *The Birth of Tragedy*), but through the acceptance of immanence. On the philosophy of *Tristan* and its origins in the thought of Feuerbach and Schopenhauer, see Sandro Barbera, *La comunicazione perfetta. Wagner tra Feuerbach e Schopenhauer* (Pisa: Jacques e i suoi quaderni, 1984), 87ff.

79. Cf. *Thus Spoke Zarathustra*, IV, "The Sleepwalker's Song, § 10 (eKGWB/Za-IV-Nachtwandler-10) and III, "Before Sunrise" (eKGWB/Za-III-Sonnen).

80. "IV Conclusion: In Genoa: Oh my friends. Do you understand this 'and yet'? —— " eKGWB/NF-1885,42[3]. My trans. See also eKGWB/NF-1878,27[9].

CHAPTER SIX

1. Nietzsche to Malwida, September 3, 1877, eKGWB/BVN-1877,622.

2. He is currently in Saint Moritz.

3. Nietzsche to Elizabeth, July 12, 1879, eKGWB/BVN-1879,866. My trans.

4. Nietzsche to Malwida, May 12, 1887, eKGWB/BVN-1887,845. My trans.

5. Cf. Berta Schleicher, *Malwida von Meysenbug. Ein Lebensbild zum hundertsten Geburtstag der Idealistin* (Berlin: Schuster & Loeffler, 1917), 110.

6. Malwida von Meysenbug, *Individualitäten*, 40–41. My trans. "Alles Vergängliche / Ist nur ein Gleichnis" are two lines from the "Chorus Mysticus" that concludes Goethe's second *Faust* (lines 12104–05).

7. "Alles Unvergängliche—das ist nur ein Gleichniss!" *Thus Spoke Zarathustra*, II, "Upon the Blessed Isles," eKGWB/Za-II-Inseln. Trans. Kaufmann, 86–87. Trans. mod. See also "On Poets": "'Since I have come to know the body better,' Zarathustra said to one of his disciples, 'the spirit is to me only a spirit so to speak; all that is "imperishable" is also merely a symbol,'" eKGWB/Za-II-Dichter. Trans. Kaufmann in *Thus Spoke Zarathustra*, 126. Trans. mod.

EDITIONS, ABBREVIATIONS, BIBLIOGRAPHY

For Nietzsche's works and correspondence, I use the German critical reference edition established by Giorgio Colli and Mazzino Montinari:

Nietzsche, Friedrich. *Werke. Kritische Gesamtausgabe*. Berlin: Walter de Gruyter, 1967–.
(Abbreviated as KGW, followed by the volume number and page number.)

——— *Briefwechsel. Kritische Gesamtausgabe*. Berlin: Walter de Gruyter, 1975–.
(Abbreviated as KGB followed by the volume number and page number.)

In most cases, I use the digital version of this edition:

Nietzsche, Friedrich. *Digitale Kritische Gesamtausgabe Werke une Briefe*, under the direction of Paolo D'Iorio. Paris: Nietzsche Source, 2009–. www.nietzschesource.org/eKGWB. (Abbreviated as eKGWB, followed by the standard reference codes indicated below.)

For example, as the normal acronym for *The Birth of Tragedy* is GT (*Die Geburt der Tragödie*), the reference code eKGWB/GT-1 refers to the first section of this work. As the acronym for the posthumous fragments is NF (*Nachgelassene Fragmente*), the reference code eKGWB/NF-1881,12 [142] refers to fragment 142 of group 12 from the year 1881. The acronym for Nietzsche's letters being BVN (*Briefe von Nietzsche*), the reference code eKGWB/BVN-1876,565 refers to letter number 565 of the year 1876. These reference codes, preceded by www.nietzschesource

.org, become the web addresses that allow one to directly consult the corresponding texts. Hence, the web addresses of the examples given above are the following:

www.nietzschesource.org/eKGWB-GT-1
www.nietzschesource.org/eKGWB-NF-1881,12[142]
www.nietzschesource.org/eKGWB/BVN-1876,565

For Nietzsche's manuscripts and original printings, I use, like Colli and Montinari, the sigla contrived by Hans Joachim Mette.[1] The facsimiles of these documents are progressively being published in:

Nietzsche, Friedrich, *Digitale Faksimile Gesamtausgabe*, under the direction of Paolo D'Iorio. Paris: Nietzsche Source, 2009–. www.nietzschesource. org/DFGA. (Abbreviated as DFGA, followed by the code of the document and the page number, for example DFGA/N-II-6,1).

In this case as well, the reference codes preceded by the address www. nietzschesource.org become the web addresses that allow one to consult the corresponding facsimiles. For example:

www.nietzschesource.org/DFGA/N-II-6,1

For the works contained in Nietzsche's personal library, I use the catalogue edited by:

Campioni, Giuliano, Paolo D'Iorio, Cristina Fornari, Francesco Fronterotta, Andrea Orsucci, and Renate Müller-Buck. *Nietzzsches persönliche Biblio-thek*. Berlin/New York: Walter de Gruyter, 2003.

In the text, unbracketed ellipses (. . .) within quotations indicate that their author expressly included these ellipses, while bracketed ellipses ([. . .]) indicate that a section of quoted text has been omitted.

For Nietzsche's works, posthumous fragments, and correspondence, the abbreviation "My trans." indicates that the translation was executed from the

---

1. Hans Joachim Mette, "Sachlicher Vorbericht zur Gesamtausgabe der Werke Friedrich Nietzsches," in Nietzsche, *Werke und Briefe. Historisch-kritische Gesamtausgabe* (München: Beck, 1933), XXXI–CXXII.

original by the English translator of the work (Sylvia Gorelick), following the guidelines of the translations by the author (Paolo D'Iorio). Translations by other translators of Nietzsche's writings are indicated by the abbreviation "Trans." followed by the name of the translator and the citation of the work. The abbreviation "Trans. mod." indicates that the English translator has modified the existing English translation to make it more faithful, in her view, to the original. English translations used include:

Nietzsche, Friedrich. *Beyond Good and Evil*. Translated by Walter Kaufmann. New York: Random House, 1966.

———. *The Birth of Tragedy*. Translated by Walter Kaufmann. New York: Random House, 1967.

———. *Daybreak: Thoughts on the Prejudices of Morality*. Translated by R. J. Hollingdale. Cambridge: Cambridge University Press, 1997.

———. *The Gay Science.* Translated by Walter Kaufmann. New York: Vintage Books, 1974.

———. *Historisch-kritische Gesamtausgabe, Briefe*. Edited by Wilhelm Hoppe. Munich: Beck, 1941.

———. *Human, All Too Human*. Translated by R. J. Hollingdale. Cambridge: Cambridge University Press, 1996.

———. *On the Genealogy of Morals* and *Ecce Homo*. Translated by Walter Kaufmann. New York: Random House, 1989.

———. *Les philosophes préplatoniciens*. Combas: Éditions de l'éclat, 1994.

———. *Thus Spoke Zarathustra*. Translated by Walter Kaufmann. New York: The Viking Press, 1954.

———. *Unmodern Observations*. Edited and translated by William Arrowsmith. New Haven: Yale University Press, 1990.

———. *Writings from the Early Notebooks*. Edited by Raymond Geuss, translated by Ladislaus Löb. Cambridge: Cambridge University Press, 2009.

The translation of texts by other authors where the name of the translator is not explicitly mentioned is always the responsibility of the English translator (Sylvia Gorelick), following the guidelines of the author (Paolo D'Iorio). A special thanks goes out, on behalf of the author and the English translator, to Thomas Bartscherer for encouraging the publication of the English edition with the University of Chicago Press.

WORKS CITED

Andler, Charles. *Nietzsche, sa vie et sa pensée*. Paris: Gallimard, 1958. 3 vols.

Associazione di studi storici sorrentini. *Sorrento e la sua storia*. Sorrento: Di Mauro, 1991.

Barbera, Sandro. *La comunicazione perfetta. Wagner tra Feuerbach e Schopenhauer*. Pisa: Jacques e i suoi quaderni, 1984.

———. *Guarigioni, rinascite e metamorfosi. Studi su Goethe, Schopenhauer e Nietzsche*. Firenze: Le lettere, 2010.

Bernoulli, Carl Albrecht. *Franz Overbeck und Friedrich Nietzsche, eine Freundschaft*. Jena: Diederichs, 1908. 2 vols.

Bloch, Peter André. "'Aus meinem Leben.' Der selbstporträtcharakter von Nietzsches frühen Lebensbeschreibungen: Selbstdialog als Selbstbefragung." *Nietzscheforschung*, 2 (1995), 61–94.

Bollinger, Andrea, and Franziska Trenkle, eds. *Nietzsche in Basel*. Basel: Schwabe, 2000.

Boltzmann, Ludwig. *Vorlesungen über Gastheorie*. Leipzig: Barth, 1896–1898. 2 vols.

Brenner, Alfred (under the pseudonym Albert Nilson). "Das flammende Herz." *Deutsche Rundschau*, 3/10 (1877), 1–11.

Busellato, Stefano, and Giuliano Campioni. *Tra la Torre e i cammelli. Nietzsche a Pisa*. Pisa: ETS, 2013.

Byron, George Gordon. *Sämmtliche Werke*. Leipzig: Wigand, 1864. 8 vols.

Campioni, Giuliano. "'Der höhere Mensch' nach dem Tod Gottes." *Nietzsche-Studien*, 28 (1999), 336–55.

———. *Les lectures françaises de Nietzsche*. Paris: PUF, 2001.

Cocchi, Igino. "Sur la naturalisation du dromadaire en Toscane." *Bulletin mensuel de la société impériale zoologique d'acclimatation*. Paris: Masson, 1858.

Cuomo, Nino. "Scoperta la villa di Nietzsche." *Match-Point*, IV/3, March 1990.

D'Annunzio, Gabriele. *Il fuoco*. Milano: Treves, 1900.

D'Iorio, Paolo. "Aucune des choses humaines n'est digne de grand sérieux. Notes sur la genèse de l'aphorisme 628 de *Choses humaines, trop humaines* de Nietzsche." *Œuvres et critique*, XXV, 1, Tübingen, 2000, 107–23.

———. "Les cloches du nihilisme et l'éternel retour du même." In *Nietzsche et le temps des nihilismes*. Edited by Jean-François Mattéi. Paris: PUF, 2005, 191–208.

———. "The Eternal Return: Genesis and Interpretation." Translated by Frank Chouraqui. *The Agonist*, 4:1 (Nietzsche Circle, Spring 2011).

———. *La linea e il circolo. Cosmologia e filosofia dell'eterno ritorno in Nietzsche*. Genova: Pantograf, 1995.

———. "Nietzsche et l'éternel retour. Genèse et interpretation," *Nietzsche*. Cahiers de l'Herne. Paris: l'Herne, 2000, 361–89.

———. "Les pensées papillons." *Genesis*, "Philosophie," texts assembled and presented by Paolo D'Iorio and Olivier Ponton, 22 (2003), 7–11.

D'Iorio, Paolo, and Olivier Ponton, eds. *Nietzsche. Philosophie de l'esprit libre. Études sur la génèse de Choses Humaines, Trop Humaines*. Paris: Éditions Rue d'Ulm, 2004.

Deleuze, Gilles, ed. *Nietzsche. Actes du colloque de Royaumont du 4 au 8 juillet 1964*. Paris: Les éditions de Minuit, 1967.

Deussen, Paul. *Erinnerungen an Friedrich Nietzsche*. Leipzig: F. A. Brockhaus, 1901.

Du Moulin-Eckart, Richard. *Cosima Wagner*. Translated by Catherine Alison Phillips. New York: Alfred A. Knopf, 1930. 2 vols.

Eco, Umberto. *Le poetiche di Joyce*. Milano: Bompiani, 2002.

Eger, Manfred. *"Alle 5000 Jahre glückt es."* Tutzing: Schneider, 2010.

Emerson, Ralph Waldo. *Die Führung des Lebens. Gedanken und Studien*. Translated by G. S. Mühlberg. Leipzig: Steinacker, 1862.

———. *Versuche*. Translated by G. Fabricius. Hannover: Carl Meyer, 1858.

Farrel Krell, David, and Donal L. Bates. *The Good European. Nietzsche's Work Sites in Word and Image*. Chicago/London: University of Chicago Press, 1997.

Fascetti Giovanni R. *I cammelli di San Rossore*. Pisa: Giardini, 1991.

Fiorentino, Alessandro. *Memorie di Sorrento. Metamorfosi di un incantesimo 1858–1948*. Napoli: Electa, 1991.

Fornari, Maria Cristina. *La morale evolutiva del gregge: Nietzsche legge Spencer e Mill*. Pisa: ETS, 2006.

Foucault, Michel, *Dits et écrits, Vol. II: 1970–1975*. Paris: Gallimard, 1994.

Fuchs, Wilhelm C. *Vulkane und Erdbeben*. Leipzig: Brockhaus, 1875.

Gautier, Théophile. *Émaux et Camées*. Paris: Gallimard, 1981.

Gilman, Sander, ed. *Conversations with Nietzsche: A Life in the Words of His Contemporaries*. Translated by David J. Parent. Oxford: Oxford University Press, 1987.

Goncourt, Edmond, and Jules Huot de. *Journal des Goncourt: Mémoires de la vie littéraire*. Paris: Charpentier, 1887. 3 vols.

———. *Pages from the Goncourt Journals*. Translated by Robert Baldick. New York: New York Review Books Classics, 2006.

Gramsci, Antonio. *Lettere dal carcere*. Torrino: Einaudi, 1947.

Gregorovius, Ferdinand. *Figuren, Geschichte, Leben und Scenerie aus Italien*. Leipzig: Brockhaus, 1856.

Gudemann, Alfred. *Imagines Philologorum*. Leipzig, 1911.

Hartmann, Eduard von. *Philosophie des Unbewussten. Versuch einer Weltanschauung*. Berlin: Carl Duncker, 1869.

Heine, Heinrich. *Sämmtliche Werke*. Homburg: Hoffmann und Campe, 1862. 21 vols.

Heller, Peter. *Von den ersten und letzten Dingen. Studien und Kommentar zu einer Aphorismenreihe von Friedrich Nietzsche*. Berlin: De Gruyter, 1972.

Hesiodos. *Hesiodea quake feruntur carmina. Ad codicum manuscriptorum et antiquorum testium fidem recensuit criticorum adjecit Arminius Koechly*. Lipsiæ: Teubneri, 1870.

His, Eduard and Hans Gutzwiller. *Friedrich Nietzsches Heimatlosigkeit. Friedrich Nietzsches Lehrtätigkeit am Basler Pädagogium 1869–1875*. Basel: Schwabe, 2002.

Hoffmann, David Marc, ed. *Nietzsche und die Schweiz*. Zurich: Offizin/Strauhof, 1994.

Iezzi, Benito. *Viaggiatori stranieri a Sorrento*. Sorrento: Di Mauro, 1989.

Janz, Curt Paul. *Friedrich Nietzsche Biographie*. München: Hanser, 1978–1979.

Joyce, James. *The James Joyce Archive*. Vol. 4: *A Portrait of the Artist as a Young Man: A Facsimile of Epiphanies, Notes, Manuscripts & Typescripts*. Prefaced and arranged by Hans Walter Gabler. New York: Garland Publishing, 1978.

———. *A Portrait of the Artist as a Young Man.* New York: Huebsch, 1916.

———. *Finnegans Wake.* London: Faber and Faber, 1939.

———. *Stephen Hero.* New York: New Directions, 1944.

———.*Ulysses.* Edited by Hans Walter Gabler. New York: Random House, 1986.

Leopardi, Giacomo. *Essays and Dialogues of Giacomo Leopardi.* Translated by Charles Edwardes. Boston: J. R. Osgood and Co., 1882.

———.*Operette morali.* Seguite da una scelta dei "Pensieri." Studio introduttivo e commento di Mario Fubini. Torino: Loescher, 1993.

Maiuri, Amedeo. *Capri: Histoire et monuments.* Roma: Instituto poligrafico e zecca dello Stato, 1981.

Mattéi, François, ed. *Nietzsche et le temps des nihilismes.* Paris: PUF, 2005.

Melchiori, Giovanni. *Joyce: il mestiere dello scrittore.* Torino: Einaudi, 1994.

Meysenbug, Malwida von. *Briefe von und an Malwida von Meysenbug.* Edited by Berta Schleicher. Berlin: Schuster & Loeffler, 1920.

———. *Im Anfang war die Liebe. Briefe an ihre Pflegtocher.* Edited by Berta Schleicher. München: Beck, 1926.

———. *Individualitäten.* Berlin: Schuster & Loeffler, 1902.

———. *Der Lebensabend einer Idealistin. Nachtrag zu den "Memoiren einer Idealistin."* Berlin: Schuster & Loeffler, 1898.

———. *Memoiren einer Idealistin.* Stuttgart: Auerbach, 1876.

———. *Phädra: Ein Roman.* Leipzig: Reissner, 1885. 3 vols.

———. *Stimmungsbilder.* Berlin und Leipzig: Schuster & Loeffler, 1905.

Mengaldo, Elisabetta. "Strategie di reticenza e demistificazione: il trattino di sospensione negli aforismi di Friedrich Nietzsche." *Studi germanici*, 1–2 (2005).

Molner, David. "The Influence of Montaigne on Nietzsche: A Raison d'Être in the Sun." *Nietzsche-Studien* 21 (1993), 80–93.

Montaigne, Michel de. *Versuche.* Translated by Herrn Peter Coste. Leipzig: Lankischens Erben, 1753. 3 vols.

Montinari, Mazzino. Critical Apparatus to *Thus Spoke Zarathustra.* In *Opere di Friedrich Nietzsche.* Vol. VI/1. Milano: Adelphi, 1968.

———.*Nietzsche lesen.* Berlin: Walter de Gruyter, 1982.

———. *Reading Nietzsche.* Translated by Greg Whitlock. Chicago: University of Illinois Press, 2003.

———. *Su Nietzsche.* Roma: Editori Riuniti, 1981.

Moretti, Franco. *Modern Epic: The World System from Goethe to García Márquez.* Translated by Quintin Hoare. London, New York: Verso, 1996.

Müller-Buck, Renate. "'Immer wieder kommt einer zur Gemeine hinzu.' Nietzsche junger Basler Freund und Schüler Albert Brenner." In *Centauren-Geburten. Wissenschaft, Kunst und Philosophie beim jungen Nietzsche.* Edited by T. Brosche, F. Gerratana, and A. Venturelli. Berlin-New York, Walter de Gruyter, 1994.

Pater, Walter Horatio. *The Renaissance: Studies in Art and Poetry.* London: Macmillan, 1877.

Pfeiffer, Ernst, ed. *Friedrich Nietzsche, Paul Rée, Lou von Salomé. Correspondance.* Translated by Ole Hansen-Løve and Jean Lacoste. Paris: PUF, 1979.

———.*Friedrich Nietzsche, Paul Rée, Lou von Salomé: die Dokumente ihrer Begegnung.* Frankfurt am Main: Insel-Verlag, 1970.

Plato. *Dialogi Secundum Thrasylli tetralogias dispositi.* Ex recognitione Caroli Friderici Hermanni. Vol. 5. Lipsiæ: Teubneri, 1862.

Ponton, Olivier. *Philosophie de la légèreté.* Berlin/New York: de Gruyter, 2007.

Rée, Paul. *Gesammelte Werke, 1875–1885.* Edited by Hubert Treiber. Berlin/New York: de Gruyter, 2004.

———. *De l'origine des sentiments moraux.* Edited by Paul-Laurent Assoun. Paris: PUF, 1982.

———. *Der Ursprung der moralischen Empfindung.* Chemnitz: Schmeitzner, 1877.

———. *The Origin of the Moral Sensations.* Edited and translated by Robin Small. Chicago: University of Illinois Press, 2003.

Santi, Georges. "Mémoire sur les chameaux de Pise." *Annales du Museum d'histoire naturelle,* no. 18. Paris, 1811.

Schlechta, Karl. *Nietzsche grosser Mittag.* Frankfurt: Klostermann, 1954.

Schleicher, Berta. *Malwida von Meysenbug. Ein Lebensbild zum hundertsten Geburtstag der Idealistin.* Berlin: Schuster & Loeffler, 1917.

Schopenhauer, Arthur. *Aphorismes sur la sagesse dans la vie.* Translated by J.-A. Cantacuzène. Paris: Alcan, 1887.

———. *Sämtliche Werke.* Leipzig: Brockhaus, 1873. 7 vols.

———. *The World as Will and Representation.* Translated by E. F. J. Payne. New York: Dover Publications, 1969. 2 vols.

Senn, Fritz. *Joyce's Dislocutions: Essays on Reading as Translation.* Baltimore and London: Johns Hopkins University Press, 1984.

Seydlitz, Reinhardt von. "Friedrich Nietzsche: Briefe und Gespräche," in Sander Gilman, ed. *Begegnungen mit Nietzsche* (Bonn: Bouvier, 1981).

Stummann-Bowert, Ruth, ed. *Malwida von Meysenbug, Paul Rée. Briefe an einen Freund.* Würzburg: Königshausen & Neumann, 1998.

Treiber, Hubert. "Beiträge zur Quelenforschung." *Nietzsche-Studien,* 27 (1998), 562.

———. "Wahlverwandtschaften zwischen Nietzsches Idee eines 'Klosters für freiere Geister' und Webers Idealtypus der puritanischen Sekte." *Nietzsche-Studien* 21 (1992), 326–62.

———. "Zur 'Logik des Traums' bei Nietzsche. Anmerkungen zu den Traumaphorismen aus MA." *Nietzsche-Studien* 23 (1994), 1–41.

Ungern-Sternberg, Isabelle von. *Nietzsche im Spiegelbild seiner Schrift.* Leipzig: Naumann, 1902.

Vivarelli, Vivetta. *L'immagine rovesciata: la letture di Nietzsche.* Genova: Matietti, 1992.

———. *Nietzsche und die Masken des freien Geistes. Montaigne, Pascal und Sterne.* Würzburg: Königshausen & Neumann, 1998.

Wagner, Cosima. *Cosima Wagner's Diaries.* Edited by Martin Gregor-Dellin and Dietrich Mack. Translated by Geoffrey Skelton. New York, London: Harcourt Brace Jovanovich, 1978–1980. 2 vols.

———. *Tagebücher.* Edited by Martin Gregor-Dellin and Dietrich Mack. München: Piper, 1976–1977. 4 vols.

Wagner, Richard. *Mein Leben.* München: List, 1963.

———. *Sämtliche Schriften und Dichtung.* Leipzig: Breitkof & Härtel, 1991. 12 vols.

Zavatta, Benedetta. *La sfida del carattere. Nietzsche lettore di Emerson.* Roma: Editori Riuniti, 2006.

INDEX